PRAISE FOR *MODERN MADNESS*:

"Terri Cheney paints a compelling picture of the mind of someone with mental illness, helping us to understand what it must feel like and causing us to sympathize with, not fear, those who suffer. Her book is a real stigma-buster—and a must-read."

—Elyn Saks, author of *New York Times* bestseller
The Center Cannot Hold: My Journey Through Madness,
2009 MacArthur Genius recipient

"I've read dozens of books and articles while researching my documentary about bipolar disorder, *Of Two Minds*. Nothing illustrates the humanity of someone living with a mental illness like Terri's stories—all told with warmth, humor, exquisite language, and unwavering honesty."

—Lisa Klein, director, *Of Two Minds* and *The S Word*

PRAISE FOR *MANIC*:

"Cheney's chilling account of her struggle with bipolar disorder brilliantly evokes the brutal nature of her disease. *Manic* . . . has heart and soul to spare."

—*People*

"Cheney's book is a gut-wrenching ride."

—*Los Angeles Times*

"Superb . . . Cheney's remarkable chronicle of her painful odyssey is as eloquent as it is brave. It is also profoundly necessary, both for her and for us."

—*Providence Journal*

"[A] gritty, vibrant memoir brings this chaotic frenzy to life . . . through disaster and despair to end in hope."

—Peter C. Whybrow, MD, author *A Mood Apart*

PRAISE FOR *THE DARK SIDE OF INNOCENCE*:

"As the father of an adult son with a severe mental illness, I found myself choking with emotion as I read Terri Cheney's riveting and illuminating account of her childhood growing up with bipolar disorder. Cheney provides us with important insights from the eyes of the most innocent among us—our very own children."

—Pete Earley, *New York Times* bestselling author of *Crazy: A Father's Search Through America's Mental Health Madness*

"Rewind the life of any adult with bipolar and you will find a childhood we would all desperately like to forget. Terri Cheney unflinchingly remembers . . . at long last, someone with the courage to break the silence."

—John McManamy, author of *Living Well with Depression and Bipolar Disorder*

MODERN
MADNESS

MODERN MADNESS

An Owner's Manual

TERRI CHENEY

hachette
BOOKS

New York

Author's note: To the best of my ability, I have re-created events, locales, people, and organizations from my memories of them. In order to maintain the anonymity of others, in some instances I have changed the names of individuals and places, and the details of events. I have also changed some identifying characteristics, such as physical descriptions, occupations, and places of residence.

Copyright © 2020 by Terri Cheney
Cover design by Amanda Kain
Cover photograph © Serghei Turcanu/GettyImages
Cover copyright © 2020 by Hachette Book Group, Inc.

Hachette Book Group supports the right to free expression and the value of copyright. The purpose of copyright is to encourage writers and artists to produce the creative works that enrich our culture.

The scanning, uploading, and distribution of this book without permission is a theft of the author's intellectual property. If you would like permission to use material from the book (other than for review purposes), please contact permissions@hbgusa.com. Thank you for your support of the author's rights.

Hachette Go, an imprint of Hachette Books
Hachette Book Group
1290 Avenue of the Americas
New York, NY 10104
HachetteGo.com
Facebook.com/HachetteGo
Instagram.com/HachetteGo

First Edition: September 2020

Hachette Books is a division of Hachette Book Group, Inc.

The Hachette Go and Hachette Books names and logos are trademarks of Hachette Book Group, Inc.

The publisher is not responsible for websites (or their content) that are not owned by the publisher.

Print book interior design by Amy Quinn.

Library of Congress Cataloging-in-Publication Data

Names: Cheney, Terri, 1959– author.
Title: Modern madness : an owner's manual / Terri Cheney.
Description: New York : Hachette Books, [2020] | Includes bibliographical references.
Identifiers: LCCN 2020014355 | ISBN 9780306846304 (hardcover) | ISBN 9780306846281 (ebook)
Subjects: LCSH: Mental illness—Popular works. | Cheney, Terri, 1959–
Classification: LCC RC460 .C46 2020 | DDC 616.89–dc23
LC record available at https://lccn.loc.gov/2020014355ISBNs: 978-0-306-84630-4 (hardcover); 978-0-306-84628-1 (ebook)

Printed in the United States of America

LSC-C

10 9 8 7 6 5 4 3 2 1

To Nancy Bacal and Dr. Geoffry White, who have kept me just sane enough all these years

CONTENTS

MODERN
MADNESS

SECTION I

Getting Started

INTRODUCTION

I WAS SITTING NEXT TO Michael Jackson, admiring his feet. Michael Jackson had surprisingly big feet—farm boy feet, with some heft to them. They didn't match the rest of him: the delicately chiseled nose, the whispery voice and waif-like persona. I was mesmerized. I kept picturing him defying the laws of gravity and motion, sliding up and back and off the floor like he was wearing invisible ice skates, ice skates with wings.

Looking back, there was indeed something extraordinary in that room, only it had nothing to do with Michael Jackson's feet. It was the mere fact that I was sitting there as one of his attorneys, representing him in a big, messy lawsuit involving one of the most successful albums of all time. That was me, all right—counselor to the stars. The voice of reason and restraint, in a gray Armani suit and a gorgeous white silk shirt I'd bought especially for the deposition, because it had these long, elegant French cuffs that would just about hide the virulent red slashes across my wrists I'd acquired from a recent suicide attempt.

Hiding had become an art form with me. I covered up the damning signs of depression with a thoroughness and frenzy that is painful to remember: pleadings prepared by flashlight in the dead of night, so no one could see how ravaged I looked; prolonged disappearances due to increasingly fictional ailments; lies piled upon tottering piles of lies. But the mania was a different story. The mania was always on full display.

I thought faster, I wrote better, I could argue the devil out of his soul when I was manic. I was glorious, bionic, at the top of my game, and I knew it and used it against anyone who came too close. Sex was mine for the asking, money and influence, too, and I owed it all to mania—including my proximity to Michael Jackson and his like. But no matter how lofty and impervious I appeared, depression could swoop in and lay me low without a word, without warning: the devil demanding a rematch.

Then it was back to hiding all over again.

Bipolar disorder wasn't a familiar term back then. It was still called manic depression, and it was something someone's batty old uncle once had. Certainly no one admitted to it by choice, and I wasn't about to start. Nobody knew what was going on with me— for a long time, I didn't even know myself. I just knew that something was terribly wrong; that something had always been terribly wrong; and that the world wasn't ready to find that out.

It took a whole lot of horrible to bring me to truth: serious run-ins with the law, immense amounts of alcohol, multiple suicide attempts, demolished relationships, financial ruin (mania's costly gift), and all the other detritus that accompanies a severe mental illness. I finally grew desperate enough to seek help, and after nearly a decade was awarded a diagnosis. But that did little to stop the entropy. I wound up in a mental hospital at UCLA, for three unimaginably long years and multiple rounds of electroshock therapy. That's when everything really started.

It was a frightening, at times mournful and demoralizing place: gray walls, gray faces, the omnipresent sound of doors being locked. I remember looking around me, wondering why nobody seemed to be getting well. Even the brightest, most impressive patients struggled, often in tears, to describe their pain. The less advantaged simply lapsed into a zombie-like silence. I felt suffocated by all the things that weren't being said, especially by me. Then one day it dawned on me. It wasn't the patients' fault. They simply didn't have a vocabulary for their illness. Why should they? Mania, suicide, psychosis—such things were hardly the stuff of polite conversation. None of us knew how to express ourselves because mental illness was a long, inarticulate howl. It needed a voice. It needed words.

And so, to save myself, I started to write. I wrote down everything I knew about bipolar disorder: the symptoms, the treatments, the various theories of origin. I read everything I could lay my hands on, even attended Grand Rounds lectures with the doctors. Then I threw away all the clinical stuff and wrote what it felt like inside my own body, how the illness skewed my view of the world. Seven years later, I emerged with a book called *Manic*.

Never in a million years could I have expected how favorable the response to *Manic* would be. It catapulted to the *New York Times* bestseller list within a month. It was optioned by HBO for a TV series and translated into eight foreign languages. I was deluged by messages from people all over the world, asking me for advice, inviting me to speak, begging me for comfort, and always, always, telling me their own stories. During those proverbial fifteen minutes, I was the poster child for bipolar disorder. For the very first time in my life, I was no longer hiding—I was out, in a very big way.

But my story doesn't end there. I didn't stop being bipolar, just because I'd tasted some success. For sanity's sake, I've had to make some sweeping changes. I've stopped practicing law to write full time and act as a mental health advocate, in order to satisfy my need to do something worthwhile and lessen the stress that had kindled my illness into full flame. But the biggest change by far has been my willingness to accept that I have a condition that isn't yet curable, and that may require a lifetime of treatment.

I don't always see this as a liability. I recognize the tremendous impact bipolar disorder has had on my life, for richer or poorer, and there is a surprising amount of richer in that equation. Without it,

I doubt I would possess those qualities I truly like in myself, like creativity, empathy, and an outsider's eye. It gives me great joy to say this: after all these years, all this suffering, this incandescent struggle, I've finally reached a point, not only of acknowledgment, but of ownership. This is what happened to me. This is my truth.

My story is bigger than bipolar disorder, though. I've come to realize that I belong to a much vaster community: the mentally ill. Regardless of the particular diagnosis, we are all dealing with divergent experience, a life beyond the norm. Stigma encompasses all of us, as do pressing issues with relationships, coping strategies, etc. That's why I've aimed this book at the broader target of "madness," a word I know may be controversial, but that I frankly adore. It assumes a spark of genius, a familiarity with things not quite of this commonplace world.

I recognize, from the countless heartfelt stories and questions I've been privy to over the years, just how complicated and frightening mental illness can be, for everyone concerned. We all need explanations, illustrations, analysis, instructions on how to build a better life in the face of exceptional challenge. Hence, this owner's manual—and I hope it can provide some of that for those who are seeking solace. This includes not only individuals with mental health issues but also the people who love and sometimes want to strangle them; the health care professionals trying to help; and the millions of other people whose lives are affected by mental illness in one form or another and don't understand what it is, or more important, what the hell to do about it. I offer this book to you.

The biggest advantage I can claim as a storyteller is that I've been there and I know the terrain. I write what I know, and I know I've been lucky. I should be dead a dozen times over, yet something has conspired to let me act as a witness to my inexplicable survival. But then, I'm no stranger to amazing events; I've met quite a few on my travels.

Take the phenomenon in that long-ago conference room. The wonder isn't how Michael Jackson could dance like an angel on farm boy feet. It's that I'm still alive to write about that moment, all these many years later, with some degree of compassion for the young woman who sat at that conference table, tugging at her shirt cuffs to hide her scars. There was a lot of peculiar talent in that room, and not all of it belonged to Michael Jackson.

The time has come to own it.

SECTION II

System Overview

MANIA

*"One must still have chaos in oneself to be
able to give birth to a dancing star."*
—Friedrich Nietzsche (1844–1900)

— — —

The latest edition of the psychiatric bible, the *Diagnostic and
Statistical Manual of Mental Disorders* ("DSM-5"), describes mania as "a distinct period of abnormally and persistently elevated,
expansive, or irritable mood and abnormally and persistently
goal-directed behavior or energy." Clinical symptoms include

- Inflated self-esteem or grandiosity;
- A decreased need for sleep;
- Pressured speech or talking more than usual;
- Racing thoughts;
- Flights of ideas;
- Distractibility; and
- Engaging in risky behaviors, like unrestrained buying sprees
  and sexual indiscretions.

Mania used to be defined by the American Psychiatric Association as "excessive involvement in pleasurable activities . . . ," which sounds fabulous, until you get to the end of the phrase: "that have a high potential for painful consequences." That's one of the problems with mania—it starts out feeling so great, you never think about how it might end.

— — —

JOURNEYS THAT TAKE YOU TOO FAR, TOO FAST

Only Monday, and already it was a lost week. The piles of important and neglected papers on my desk had copulated in the night, producing even more piles. My house was a shambles—how long since I'd cleaned it?—and I was too tired to snap to and take charge. I went to bed cranky and frustrated. But when I woke the next morning I felt it—that dazzling surge of energy that makes me long for a project, any project, to devour. I ripped through the tedious papers, making brilliant observations and uncanny deductions, signing my name with a flourish. True, my handwriting was on the verge of illegible, and the words just kept coming and coming at me till I had to scream to make them stop—but still. The whole mess was over and done with, in less time than it takes to squish a gnat.

Then I turned to the house. Not a speck of dirt or dust could escape my darting eyes. I Lysoled and Windexed and Pledged and Febrezed until the entire place reeked of ammonia and pine. Such a heavenly scent—proof positive that whatever else may be wrong with me, I am irrefutably clean. The rewards began to diminish, of course, when the whole house was so spotless I couldn't find anything else to polish or dust. That's when I got out the Q-tips, so I could get to that last tiny crevice inside the microwave. That's when I found the magnifying glass, so I could kneel down on the bathroom floor and inspect the grout between the shower tiles. That's when I ripped off my rubber gloves and scrubbed everything I'd already scrubbed with raw bleach, until my knuckles were bloody.

That's when clean began to feel dirty.

I had to get dressed and get out of there, away from the suffocating fumes—some place big enough to let me breathe. I'd stripped off all my clothes long ago because they constricted my movements;

and I wasn't quite high enough to go outside naked, although it made a lot more sense to me than putting on something I'd only have to remove again later. My tousled hair was up in a ponytail, my face and body covered in sweat. But my mirror lied as sweetly and smoothly as a best friend.

"You look so beautiful," it cooed. "You look better now than when you were thirty. Any man would be lucky to get you." So in lieu of my normally clean-scrubbed looks, I lavished my eyes with thick black mascara, swiped on a vampier lipstick, a bolder blush. I painted my toenails in Pirate's Blood red, then showcased them in the cruelest pair of stilettos I own. Jeans I'd bought two sizes ago were somehow slithered into. The woman in the mirror gazed back at me with complete and absolute approbation.

I shudder to think what I must have looked like, all dolled up for the kill. I live in L.A., so I've seen my fair share of women who refuse to acknowledge their age. It's never pretty. Nor am I, when I look this way and act like a tigress on the prowl. It's embarrassing, and it isn't me, except it's wearing my face and fingerprints—which means I'm ultimately responsible for any havoc that may ensue.

That didn't deter me. I got in my car and sped down to the Sunset Strip, which may be the only place in town where I truly belong when I'm manic. It's even gaudier than I am, and the flashing throb of the neon signs is music to my heart. I cruised the Strip looking for diversion, feeling the energy shimmer up like heat from the road. I started to drive faster, weaving in and out of the heavy traffic, ignoring the horns that kept honking at me. I opened the windows and let the hot night air flow through my car. It ruffled my hair, so I stopped to smooth it in the mirror, and a car slammed into me from behind.

I was livid, until I saw how handsome the driver was. He was very angry—"What the hell do you think you're doing, stopping right in the middle of traffic like that?"—but I summoned up my most dulcet voice, confessed that it was all my fault, and would he like to join me for a drink while we exchanged insurance information? The Chateau Marmont was just a block away . . . He looked surprised, but agreed. I can't remember what happened several dirty martinis after that, only that I woke up somewhere in the Hollywood Hills and my manic bravado had completely deserted me. I looked at his sleeping face on the pillow and wondered who and how and now what?

Quickly tiptoeing out, I found my way back down to the Strip and eventually back to my house. My fickle mirror didn't welcome me this time. I looked just like the mess I was: mascara smeared around my eyes, hair a rat's nest, clothes rumpled—what remained of them. My underwear was missing, or had I even worn any that night? Once again, she—that harridan who steals my face—had triumphed, leaving me feeling small and lost and terrified.

I tried to recall exactly what had happened, but it all blurred together in a messy montage. The only reliable evidence I had was my car's mangled bumper and a Chateau Marmont cocktail napkin in my purse, bearing some indecipherable manic squiggles. Not much, but it sparked my memory. Bits and pieces slowly came back to me—his lips, my purrs, those elusive panties—and I burned with shame. *Maybe a shower would help*, I thought. As I stepped in, I noticed how immaculate it was: crystal clear glass, gleaming chrome, shining tiles. But it didn't matter. No matter how hard I tried—and I try awfully hard, every time—I just couldn't scrub myself clean.

— — —

JUDGMENT DAY

When I accepted the offer, I was perfectly sane. It seemed like an excellent opportunity, a career building block, although the prestige far outweighed the money. I'd been asked to speak to 350 federal judges in Oklahoma about mental illness and the law. I knew a lot about mental illness, but as a lawyer I'd limited my practice to the very narrow field of entertainment and intellectual property. So I wasn't sure what, if anything, I had to say about the topic. But the conference was over a month away, and I figured if I could prepare for trial in a month, I could handle this.

For a brief, uneasy moment I remembered what high-pressure trial prep always did to me. But I was so much better now and besides, I was thrilled to be invited. A lot of my cases had been in federal court, and I was in thrall to its mystique. Federal judges are the rock stars of the judiciary. Unlike state court judges, they're appointed for life, so they operate in a realm beyond censure or esteem; they can be as nasty, or as nice, or as eccentric as they damn well please. But for all its perks and glamour, this tenure comes with an awesome responsibility: they hold the Constitution in their hands.

For the next two weeks, I walked around in an ambient glow of anticipation. I treated myself to a new black suit in a more conservative cut than I already owned. I liked how professional it made me look—it erased all the years of mental hospitals and suicide attempts and multiple DUIs and electroshock therapy. In that suit, I had no sordid history. I blended in with the rest of society—better yet, the serious and sober part.

Ten days before the conference, I finally overcame my deeply engrained habit of procrastination and buckled down to research. The first night, I worked until midnight. The next night, until 2 a.m. The next until 4 a.m., and then I just stopped sleeping. I didn't worry that this would make me manic. I felt fine. Better than fine—I felt fabulous. In fact, the loss of sleep didn't hurt my performance at all: with each successive hour I grew more and more creative. Thoughts bloomed like roses; I simply had to reach out and pluck them.

The central thrust of my speech was about the increasingly urgent need for diversion programs and mental health courts. Normally, I wouldn't find this very scintillating, although I knew it was an important and worthy subject. But I was so enmeshed in my beautiful words and facts and figures, I couldn't imagine anyone not being moved to tears by what I had to say. I thought it was surely the best speech ever written on the subject, and was certain to rouse the judges to action. Why, who knew what impact I'd have on the nation?

With the speech out of the way, all I had to do was pack. I pulled the black suit out of my closet and shuddered with revulsion. Seriously? I was going to wear that? It looked like I was attending the funeral of somebody I didn't like very well. Emergency action was required—I needed edgy, radical styling that shouted "success." Simply put, I needed Barney's.

When I'm not manic, I never go into Barney's. I don't even look at the windows. It's so high-end it both awes and repulses me. But I quickly found my desire: an Ozbek original, the saleswoman said in a hushed tone as she gingerly handed it over. I didn't know who Ozbek was, but the suit was certainly original. It was silvery black with long, swooping sleeves and a plunging neckline and narrow pants that were notched at the ankle. It looked sexy with nothing on underneath, but I bowed to the occasion and bought a wisp of white shirt.

I had a mild coronary when the saleswoman told me the price. My entire wardrobe wasn't worth that. But what was money? I'd always make more. After all, 350 federal judges were eagerly awaiting my wisdom, and who knew where that would lead? I walked out of Barney's on a cloud of confidence.

Somewhere high over Arizona I got a headache. The lack of sleep was beginning to prey on my nerves. I took two Benadryl, hoping they would soothe my throbbing head and knock me out, but they did just the opposite: they made me wide awake, wired, and angry. Angry that the judges were putting me through such an ordeal: all the angst, the preparation, the anxiety, the expense. Who did they think they were, anyway?

I thought back to the federal magistrate who had handled all the pretrial issues in my big Michael Jackson case. I constantly had to appear before him, usually to defend Michael's inability to attend some legal proceeding. He'd rip into me in front of opposing counsel and the rest of the courtroom. "Look, Little Missy," he'd say. "I know your firm, and I'm sure they wouldn't approve of such B.S." It was hard enough being the only woman amongst all the male attorneys; "Little Missy" made it almost impossible.

The gall of them, that murder of crows, to call me "Little Missy" and then expect me to meekly bow to their demands. They wanted me to opine on mental illness and the law? Fine. I jettisoned diversion programs on the spot. Instead, I'd give them a rip-roaring example of how the law—their precious, high-minded, beautiful law—had cruelly trampled on the rights of the mentally ill. In short, I'd tell them the story of me.

I spent the rest of the night drafting a new speech, ignoring any qualms about changing the topic without notice. Then I showered and tried to camouflage my pallor and the purple bruises under my eyes. I pulled out the new suit and poured myself into it. It looked a whole lot funkier in Oklahoma than it had in Beverly Hills, and I felt a twinge of concern, but only a twinge. I figured I could get away with anything so long as I told them I used to practice entertainment law.

The conference hall was echoey huge, and cold as court. It was odd, I'd expected the judges to be wearing their robes, but they weren't and that disturbed me. I was nervous when I started to speak but quickly warmed to my story. I told them how I was jailed for driving under the influence of prescription medication. I told them about my repeated requests to take my dangerously overdue psychiatric drugs and to contact my attorney and psychiatrist—all of which were blatantly ignored. Then I told them about the guard's reaction when I lost my temper and demanded a phone call:

"She was all over me, all two hundred pounds of her. She forced my head to the floor. It was sticky with what I later realized was my own blood. She jammed one knee against my back, and started hitting. Not with her fist, with the club that hung by her side. I was shaking so badly I don't know how she managed to land a solid blow, but she must have been thoroughly trained because my ribs were exploding, one after another, a most thorough and systematic attack . . . Nothing has ever been the same for me since that endless moment on the cold stone floor. Nothing ever will be again. I know now that I am touchable, that I am not immune."

I implored the judges to appreciate the consequences of such treatment on an extremely vulnerable population. I told them about my own resulting suicidality, and how difficult it's been for me simply to stay alive since. To my surprise, I started tearing up. It *had* been hard, harder than they could possibly know. It suddenly seemed very important that these highly influential people understood the struggle of all those like me. I stopped being worried about changing my speech. This was the story I needed to tell, and maybe even the one they needed to hear.

I folded up my pages and let my final words linger in the air. The judges were eerily silent. Then it began in the back, a ripple that quickly spread through the room and grew louder with each passing second. It couldn't be, but it was: applause. To my astonishment, people began to get to their feet, until the entire room was standing. The last thing in the world I ever expected was a standing ovation.

I fielded questions from all sides—good questions that showed the judges had really listened—until the next session was due to start, and the auditorium was almost clear. Then a tall man with a craggily handsome face came up to me and took my hand. "I want you to know how much your speech meant to me," he said. "I tried to kill myself five months ago, and it gave me hope to hear that you've been suicidal, too. As a judge, I don't get to talk about it with anyone. Now I don't feel so alone." I'm sure I was breaking protocol, but I reached out and hugged him until I could feel his trembling stop.

The federal judges would be the first to say it: Sometimes justice is served in the oddest ways. Mania can bring such strange gifts with it—in this case, a genuine passion that ignited minds and moved people. But obviously, it all could have gone sideways; one can never really predict what the impact will be. It was a thought to ponder at great length someday . . . But at that moment, what I desperately needed was to lie down on crisp cotton sheets, order room service, and absorb what had happened. Then maybe, finally, to sleep.

— — —

THE BIG CON

A few weeks ago, for no cause at all, I found myself elated, enraptured, and obviously manic. Terrific, right? But here was the hitch: I had plans to meet a former boss for lunch, and I wanted to pass as "normal." I'd done my best to hide behind a tightly clenched professionalism back when I used to work with him, and I wasn't sure what he knew about the real me. Even if he did know I have bipolar disorder, I wanted him to think it was well under control. Ten years had passed, and I was still trying to hoodwink him with my aplomb. It's funny how our poses cling to us.

So rather than the flashy colors and big bold prints that were begging to escape my closet, I wore a classic uniform (classic, at least, for L.A.): a tailored black jacket, white shirt, and jeans—not skanky skinny jeans, either, just a clean tapered cut. On my way out of the house, though, I grabbed a pair of neon cats' eyes shades, to satisfy my lust for self-expression. But I took them off when I reached the restaurant. *Such amazing self-control*, I thought. I'd have no problem at all with lunch.

Then again . . . I've been found out before. No matter how hard I work to keep my mania a secret, people who know me well often guess the truth. I hate this. It's deeply humiliating to be told that I'm manic, just as bad as being told I'm drunk or sloppy or out of control. And then it starts: the hovering, the unspoken disapproval, the buzzkill.

Until recently, I never understood how my friends saw through my facade. But then I saw the film *House of Games*, about confidence men. It seems con men know how to read their marks because they watch them closely for "tells." We all have tells: unconscious movements or facial expressions or subtle tics that give away what we're feeling. Apparently, my friends have learned my tells.

But maybe if I camouflaged them really well . . . Why hadn't I thought of this before? I'd do the exact opposite of what I was feeling. I'd play an upside-down version of myself: quivering on the edge of depression, instead of a manic high. Dysphoric, not euphoric; or at the very least, extremely unemotional. It would be like a game of hide-and-seek, except only I would know what was hidden. Instead of dreading the lunch, I now looked forward to it with a fiendish glee. Hah! This was going to be fun.

He was waiting for me in a booth by the window, in his ubiquitous gray gabardine suit. I wondered if he ever wore anything else. He still reminded me of a wizened, near-sighted clerk who looked nothing like the fierce litigator he really was. He stood up, and there was an awkward pause where I didn't know how to greet him. I wanted to say, "Hey there, Georgie boy," and give him a great big hug. But I held out my hand and gave his a firm shake. "Nice to see you, George," I said.

We small-talked about people we used to know. I'd never realized that George was such a gossipmonger, but then he'd never seemed so fascinating to me before. (When I'm manic, every dullard is bewitching.) After the waiter took our order, George just kept on chatting away, but I'd stopped listening by then because I didn't like how his silverware was arranged. Mania demands perfection, down to the teeniest-tiniest detail. His fork and knife were okay, but the spoon was askew.

I was aching to reach out and straighten it. All of me wanted to, but I sat on my hands and endured the godawful asymmetry. To anyone who might be watching, I no doubt looked still as a statue. But I was jiggling my legs under the table so hard I accidentally smacked it with my knee, spilling my coffee all over George. I apologized profusely, but *gabardine's easy to dry clean*, I thought, and he must have a million more of those suits. As he wiped the coffee off his pants with his napkin, I reached over surreptitiously and moved his spoon.

We got through the appetizers okay, but by the time our entrées arrived I noticed that George was staring at me. *Damn it*, I thought. *He knows something's up.* But instead he said, "I never noticed before that your eyes are green," which was the most personal thing he'd said to me in all the years we'd known each other. I should have been pleased, but it was another tell: when I'm manic, my hazel eyes glow yellow-green, like a cat's. I quickly narrowed them into the hostile squint of depression.

"I'm sorry, did I offend you?" George asked.

Rapid-fire speech also gives me away, and a spurt of words was trying hard to escape: "Of course not, don't be silly, tell me more about my green eyes," I longed to say. But I swallowed my eagerness, lowered my vocal register, and . . . talked . . . like . . . this. "Nooo, not at alll," I said, in a dulled-down drawl.

The check came, and we both reached for it. He was more insistent than I was, and to disguise my manic aggressiveness, I gave in and let him pay. "Ah, I remember now," he said as he took out his wallet. "You never were quite tough enough." We said our goodbyes, and I was politely furious. He might be a junkyard dog in the courtroom, I thought, but he knew nothing about tough. Tough was hiding your tells, living against your instincts. Tough was pulling off the endless con.

MANIC CHEAT SHEET

Back when I had money, I developed a lovely bad habit of dropping out of sight and reemerging in Santa Barbara. I didn't tell my friends or my bosses where I was going. I just disappeared into the sunset over Pacific Coast Highway, listening to Joseph Campbell's "Follow Your Bliss" audiotape and scheming how I could quit my job. I was usually manic when I did this, or on the brink of becoming so.

I remember one time pulling into the sweeping driveway of the Biltmore Hotel. The pink bougainvillea that draped the entrance rustled in the ocean breeze, welcoming me. "Aaaah," I sighed, as the valets and bellhops swarmed my car. A disturbingly handsome young man, dark-eyed and deeply tanned in a spruce white uniform, opened the car door for me. Mindful of his gaze, I extricated myself slowly, holding his hand for balance. I felt like a princess making an entrance—until I gracefully tripped, landing splat on the cobblestones. My purse flew open and all its contents went sprawling out over the drive.

The valet did his best to recover my things, even scrambling under my car to retrieve my lipstick. Despite his efforts, a few papers were lost to the wind. *It was probably just something related to work*, I thought. Good riddance. I tried to tip him, but he refused. "Please," I insisted, but he shook his head. "It's my pleasure," he said, as he ushered me into the lobby.

"You're awfully kind," I said, feeling that old familiar risk-taking tingle. "Can I buy you a drink when you're free?" (I'm so practiced at asking men out for drinks when I'm manic, I could lecture on it at Vassar.)

"I'll be off in an hour," he said.

"Terrific! I'll meet you in the lounge."

I went to my room to unpack. Something was missing, but I couldn't say what. Perfume? Check. Mascara? Check. Stilettos? Check, and check. I slipped them on, with a sexier dress and some racy new lingerie. But the feeling continued to nag at me: What had I forgotten? Was it important? Would I need it? Oh well, I shrugged. Whatever it is, I can buy it in the gift shop later.

I went to the lounge, ordered myself a tequila sunrise, and settled in to wait. The bar was busy—lovers and tourists cooing over the magnificent view of the ocean. I glanced in that direction: a sunset. Pretty, but I'd seen it before. I was more interested in the view of me. I took great care to arrange myself on the stool: a little leg, a glimpse of shoulder, just indiscreet enough to be noticed.

A man at the bar came over to me. Another dashing devil, only this one had blue eyes and was wearing a crisp white shirt with epaulets. Having dated a pilot once, I knew what those four bars meant: a captain.

"Quite a view," he said.

"That?" I waved my hand at the panorama.

"That, among other things," he said. He looked down at my empty glass. "Can I buy you a sunrise?" he said, and I giggled. It sounded salacious to me, but then most things do when I'm manic.

"Maybe," I said. "What's your name?"

"Dan," he said. "And you are . . . ?"

I put a finger to my lips. "Incognito," I whispered. "So tell me, which airline are you with?"

"I fly corporate," he said. I've never once dated for money, but still: visions of Lear Jets and Gulfstreams flitted before my eyes. At the slightest whim, we might be off to Acapulco or Paris or wherever for the weekend. Imagine all the art I could see, the tales I could tell, the glitz and the glamour of a jet-setting life . . .

"Yes, you may buy me a drink, Captain Dan." I heard the rhythmic lilt in my voice, and for a moment, I felt uneasy but I wasn't sure why.

He drank Glenlivet, as all men should. I kept to tequila but switched to shots on his dare. Probably not a wise idea: Alcohol is trouble enough on its own, but it instantly kindles my mania, as if a match had been held to my brain. I downed another shot, and fire exploded inside me: oranges and violets and flamingo pinks, as if I'd swallowed the sunset instead.

I felt a hand on my shoulder and turned around: the handsome valet. The two men immediately started sizing each other up. I got in between their glares and said, "This is my old friend, um—I'm sorry, I don't know your name."

"David," he said.

"Dan, meet David," I said. Or should it be David, meet Dan? It was getting awfully hot in there; droplets of sweat snaked down my back, and I was suddenly flushed and confused. Why were they both wearing white uniforms? Should I be wearing one, too?

"Give me a minute to change," David said. "Hotel policy."

"Ooh, are we breaking a rule?" I said.

"Not yet," he said, and he winked. I laughed, but Captain Dan didn't seem amused.

I watched David leave, and wished I could go with him. His eyes were so dark, they looked like they were rimmed with kohl. They were the eyes of an Arabian prince. I pictured myself swathed in colorful silks, riding bareback with him across desert dunes. Pretty boys were feeding me sweet fresh dates and waving palm fronds across my body to keep me cool . . .

A jazz combo started playing, annoying and loud. The music inside my head was so much nicer. "It's suffocating in here," I said. "Let's leave a note with the bartender so David can find us." I scribbled two words on a cocktail napkin and handed it to Captain Dan. He looked at it, quizzically. "The ocean?" he said.

"Yes, let's go for a swim. I need to clear my head."

"But I don't have a bathing suit."

"Neither do I."

It didn't take him long to settle our bill after that. When we stepped outside, the night had turned cool and windy. "I need to get my pashmina," I said. "Back in a flash." It didn't occur to me how absurd this was: as if a small silky shawl could keep the chill off my wet, naked body. Captain Dan leaned against a pillar and lit a cigarette. I spotted David coming up the path behind him. I wondered if I should stay and soothe the tension, but then I figured, it would be so much more fun to watch the sparks fly.

I hurried to my room and grabbed my pashmina. A paper came fluttering out from its folds—a page from a legal pad. *I'll deal with it later*, I thought, and started to put it back into my suitcase when I saw the title, in red ink and all caps: "WARNING! READ IMMEDIATELY!" *Uh-oh*, I thought. This can't be fun. But I sat down on the bed, smoothed out the well-worn paper, and read:

"If you suspect you're getting manic, you probably are. You MUST obey these ten sacred rules:

1. Don't change into something sexier. Wear granny panties and flats.
2. Don't make friends with strangers. They're strangers.
3. Don't drink anything but iced tea—Lipton's, not Long Island.
4. Don't get naked, except to shower. Alone. And don't shave your legs.
5. Don't try to beguile attractive men. Or attractive women. Or cops.

6. Don't pull out your credit card for any reason, except if necessary to post bail.

7. Don't call or text or email ever—except, as noted, for bail.

8. Don't cut your hair short. You aren't Audrey Hepburn.

9. Don't quit your day job.

10. Don't follow your bliss."

My manic cheat sheet. I kept multiple copies of it with me at all times—in my glove compartment, my suitcase, my briefcase, my purse. That must have been the paper that flew away when I fell. I'm supposed to read it every day, but frankly, I forget to when I start to feel high. Or more likely, I don't wanna. But those rules had saved me countless times, from danger and improvidence and self-sabotage and worse. I carried them for a reason, and I reluctantly admitted that I ought to heed their advice.

Thinking wistfully of the two men waiting for me, I kicked off my heels and slipped off my dress and put on the thick white terry cloth robe provided by the hotel. How perfect: my very own white uniform. I locked the door and shut off the lights and pretended that I hadn't done any real harm—or, at least, not too much. Was this rude? Maybe—but it was also safe.

— — —

DEPRESSION

"I felt a Funeral, in my Brain . . ."
—Emily Dickinson (1830–1886)

— — —

"Sad." "Out of sorts." "Lethargic." "Blue." Everyone thinks they know depression, but clinical depression is much more debilitating than most people can imagine. The DSM-5 outlines the following criteria for a diagnosis of major depression:

- Markedly diminished interest in all, or almost all, activities;
- Significant changes in weight or appetite;
- A slowing down of thought and reduction of physical movement;
- Fatigue or loss of energy;
- Feelings of worthlessness, or excessive or inappropriate guilt;
- Diminished ability to think or concentrate, or indecisiveness;
- Recurrent thoughts of death or suicide.

To qualify for a diagnosis, these symptoms must cause the individual significant distress or impair his functioning in social, occupational, or other important areas. They must also not be a result of substance abuse, or another medical condition.

Antidepressants are mainly aimed at improving mood and social functioning. But depression also has a profound impact on attention and memory, as well as information-processing and decision-making skills. According to the Harvard Medical School, "[These] cognitive impairment symptoms have received little attention—and haven't necessarily been the target of medications for depression." While behavioral therapies may help, further research is urgently needed to help people return to full mental functioning (https://www.health.harvard.edu/blog/sad-depression-affects-ability-think-201605069551).

That's why I have such tremendous admiration for anyone who outlasts depression—it takes exceptional courage to exist on a few faint memories of light.

— — —

EVERY DAY, EVERYDAY MIRACLES

Stare at your hairbrush. Count the bristles. Hear the clock ticking on the counter. Ignore it. The hairbrush is what matters. It's round and spiky, like an instrument of torture. Sometime in the very near future you must apply it to your scalp, not just once but over and over again. This ritual, however painful, will allow you to pass unnoticed in a crowd. You'll be coiffed, and no one will know what it took for you to brush your hair.

Everyone I know with major depression faces some version of this scenario—a pitched battle with the seemingly innocuous tasks of daily living. Grooming, washing the dishes, making the bed, etc.: all Herculean assignments. It's not surprising, given that depression saps the motivation, energy, organizational skills, and focus such activities require. When your brain is depleted, a load of laundry can feel more complicated than chaos theory.

The flip side of self-care is self-neglect, and it makes perfect sense in a blighted world. Why bother to care for yourself when you despise who you are and what you've become? This isn't a rare phenomenon at all, but like so many aspects of depression it isn't openly discussed. Again, not surprising: there's nothing more humiliating than admitting that laundry makes you suicidal.

For me, the hardest thing by far is to get into the shower. "Why don't you take a nice hot shower?" my mother would always ask me when I'd call her, crying. She might as well have said, "Why don't you go climb Everest?" Because I can't. I just can't face it.

But yesterday I had no choice. My dearest friend in all the world was in the hospital and I promised him I'd visit. He was dying; who knew if this would be my last chance? Even given these exigent circumstances, I still had to struggle with myself. What if I waited another day? Maybe I'd feel more up to it then; and maybe it wouldn't be too late. That's how difficult a simple act like showering can be when you're depressed: it makes you play chess with God.

I could at least try, I told myself, as I lay in bed imagining the impossible. The thought of that claustrophobic cell with its stabbing stream of water taunted me. "Come let me assault you," I could almost hear it hiss, and I did my best not to listen. I'm fastidious by nature, but the thought of all those gallons of water pelting my naked nerve endings was just too much to contemplate. I preferred to wear my own dirt.

But I couldn't inflict that on my friend. Days when I can't get into the shower are bound to be bad days, spent hiding in bed. Bad days are usually microcosms of bad weeks, when I avoid all human contact, resolutely ignoring the phone and attempting social invisibility. I wallow in abysmal failure then, hating my inertia but unable to overcome it. My hair gets straggly, my clothes turn rank, my skin is slick from oil and sweat. In short, I smell like depression.

So I continued to eye that damned shower. *If only*, I thought. If only I could bear that, I could bear anything. If only I could get nice and clean, I could start my life out fresh. For twenty minutes I visualized getting up, but my body didn't share the visualization: it stayed right where it was. Finally, I managed to move my foot an inch or so toward the edge of the bed. Another twenty minutes went by before I could move it any farther. Then in a burst of violent concentration, I swung my legs up and over and stood—dizzy from the sudden movement, furious that it took this much effort just to get out of bed.

I forced myself to walk into the bathroom, open the shower door, and turn on the water. I stared at it for a good long time, wondering why such a marvel of nature and engineering was my nemesis. I had to muster all my willpower to reach out and place my hand under the stream. "There now, that's not so bad," I told myself with a shudder, and I kept progressively submerging my body—wrist, forearm, elbow, shoulder—until I was accustomed to the stinging sensations against my skin.

It was agony, but it was endurable agony; sometimes endurable agony is as good as it gets. I took a deep breath and stepped in.

There are small miracles that take place every day—heroics that nobody knows about, but that are feats of glory all the same. Somewhere today a severely depressed person is getting out of bed and brushing her teeth. Somewhere someone is deciding to eat breakfast rather than commit suicide. In my house, victory looks like getting wet.

PISTOL-WHIPPED

When I was cleaning out a jammed drawer recently, I found this story from many years ago. I'd forgotten all about it. But now that I've unearthed the incident, I think it's worth remembering—if only to be grateful that it happened a long time ago, and not yesterday. Here's what I read:

I'm writing this from the very depths. From the ragged hole at the heart of hell. I've been depressed for an eternity now, or at least several weeks, and there's no glimmer of hope on the horizon. There never is, when it's this bad. When I woke up this morning, the pain was worse. I didn't think that was possible. Dante said there were only nine circles of hell. Clearly, Dante was wrong.

Today is Tuesday, and I'm supposed to go to therapy on Tuesdays. But that's impossible, so I leave a message with my doctor canceling our session. This is incredibly thoughtful of me because it's so hard to pick up the phone, then dial, then talk, then hang up the phone. The energy required to do all this depletes me, and I go back to bed.

The phone rings, and I let the machine pick it up. It's my therapist, asking if I'm okay. How percipient of him: I was crying when I left him that message. But then, I'm always crying these days. He probably thinks that's status quo. I'd like to forgive him his ignorance because long ago when I wasn't depressed, I thought he was a decent man. But he should be able to read my mind, God knows he's dissected it long enough. He should know that I'm far from okay.

I'm scared like a child left alone in the dark. There's a big black shadow looming over me. We've met before, and I know what it wants. It wants me to go on a journey with it, down and down and ever down, until we hit oblivion.

Almost a week ago, the shadow and I took a trip to a pawn shop together. It was in a seedy part of Beverly Hills, which meant it wasn't exactly skid row, but it wasn't Rodeo Drive, either. There was a staleness to the air inside—maybe just a cigarette haze, but to me it smelled like sulfur. I told the man behind the counter about a recent rash of burglaries in my area. I told him I felt I needed protection. He took a good look at me, up and down, from my sleek bob to my tasseled loafers.

"I think I have just the thing for you," the man said. "Small, so you can carry it in your purse. But lethal, if needs be." He fiddled with a jangly bunch of keys, reached down and pulled something out of a drawer. Then he gently set it down on the counter, on a black velvet cloth, just like they do at Tiffany's.

It was beautiful, a work of great craftsmanship and terrifying to behold: a small mother-of-pearl-handled pistol. I picked it up gingerly. It fit the palm of my hand.

"It's so light," I said. "Are you sure it will work?"

The man smiled. "It's perfect for your needs." I wondered how much he had guessed, but before I could even start to worry he played the ultimate salesman's card. He reached down and pulled out a mirror. "Just look," he said. "It suits you, don't you think?"

That settled it. I looked like a femme fatale from a '30s film noir. All I lacked was a gauzy black veil and elbow-length gloves. I pulled a credit card out of my purse and didn't even ask how much.

"I'll take a deposit now," he said. "But there's a brief waiting period before you can take her home." Then he told me some stuff about paperwork, and proof of residency, and forms of I.D., and other annoying incidentals. I waited for him to ask me about my mental status, ready to lie through my teeth, but he didn't. The shadow and I linked arms as we left the store.

Since then, bad as the depression's been, I haven't tried to hurt myself. I haven't sharpened knives or counted out pills. That would be amateur hour. Instead, I've counted down the days, and crossed them off the calendar with a big red X.

It's Tuesday. The waiting period ends Wednesday. One more day.

My damn phone rings again. I contemplate not picking it up because I already know who it will be. Then I'll have to hear it one more time: the old saw about the hospital. Out of spite, I decide to make him wait. I answer on the very last ring because it might be the last ring, ever.

"I'm going to check up on you every hour between patients," he says. "Will you promise me you'll pick up the phone?" His usually mellifluous, careful voice sounds funny, kind of hoarse, as if he has a cold.

"Are you okay?" I ask.

"No, Terri, I'm not okay," he says. "I'm very worried about you. I wish you would listen to me about the hospital. You shouldn't have to suffer like this."

I can feel the chunk of ice around my heart crack just a bit, just enough to let that in. In a way, he's even scarier than the shadow. What if he really does care? It doesn't matter what the pearl-handled pistol does to me. But what will it do to him, when I use it?

"I'll think about it," I say, for what feels like the hundredth time. Then I hang up the phone and I wait. An hour goes by so slowly when you're waiting to be loved. Sure enough, in fifty-five minutes the phone rings again. I answer more quickly this time.

"How are you doing?" he asks.

"The same," I say, but as is often the case in therapy, I'm not quite telling the truth. Something is shifting; something feels different. I wait another fifty-five minutes, until he calls again. And again. And again.

There's no way he can know it, but with every one of his calls, tomorrow gets a little farther away. The depression seems so much bigger to me now: It's not only my own despair, it belongs to everyone who's ever loved me. Everyone who will torment themselves with what they might have said or done, if only . . . The pain will all be over for me, but for them, it will just be beginning.

He calls me again, right on the dot. "How are you doing?" he says.

"I—um—I think I should tell you something," I stutter. "I really don't want to, but I think you should know. A couple of weeks ago, I . . ."

In a pawn shop in the seedier part of Beverly Hills, a pearl-handled pistol still waits.

THREE ENORMOUS WORDS

Years ago, on one of my very first days as a lawyer, a boozy old partner strolled into my office. He smelled like good scotch and a bad cigar, and he came a little too close to my desk.

"Scared?" he said, and I nodded.

"You should be. Litigation is hell."

I didn't know what to say to that. Then he came even closer, and I started to sweat. But he slapped a book down on my desk.

"You'll find all the answers you need in that," he said. Then he meandered back out. I don't think I ever saw him again, but it was a big firm, and sometimes people got lost.

I figured it was *Nimmer on Copyright*, or the *Code of Civil Procedure*, or something like that. But he surprised me: it was Sun Tzu's *The Art of War*. And the old man was right: the answers were in there.

I have tremendous respect for battle: Like so many bipolar people, I've always been a fighter. I've had to be—I was born with a mind that fought back. Which doesn't mean I've always been brave. Far from it. My courage is the kind that comes out when I'm pinned against a wall; it's born of desperation. But I'd be a fool if I weren't afraid. I know all too well what's inside me, just waiting to get out.

The world gets very spooky when I'm on the verge of a depression. It's like a carnival after hours—full of half-glimpsed terrors and half-heard noises, evil vapors swirling in the air. Take the other night: I was driving through an unfamiliar alley when, without any warning, an enormous man brandishing a pitchfork suddenly appeared to my left. I stomped on the gas to get away from him and bang! I drove straight into a pothole, crunching my bumper. Terrified, I looked back in my rearview mirror, but the enormous man hadn't moved an inch. He was still standing in the exact same place, pitchfork poised at the exact same angle.

I squinted and looked harder. Damn. You know you're in a fragile state of mind when a mural scares the bejeezus out of you.

It's always that way when depression is looming. I startle at the slightest sound. I shiver when the wind barely touches my skin. I'm afraid of all sorts of nameless things, and some things that have very definite names. Dying. Dying alone. Dying alone in a windowless room. I could go on, but what's the point? We all know the night. Only some of us carry it with us into the daytime.

Sometimes, of course, it's completely reasonable to be anxious. You only need a whiff of the news to realize that these are perilous times, worthy of a fair dollop of worry. But there's no fear like the fear of depression returning. It's weightless, disembodied, intangible. Quite literally, it's all in the mind. But that doesn't lessen its horror. How can I conquer it, when it's so ephemeral? How do I fight an invisible fear?

I do what the old man told me. I go back to *The Art of War*, and its seminal lesson: know thy enemy. "If you know the enemy and know yourself," Sun Tzu said, "you need not fear the result of a hundred battles." So when my body revolts—it hurts to blink, my lungs protest against every breath—I know who's come to visit. When I get global—everything is awful, the whole world is against me—I know what's going on. At that point, the most valuable thing I can say to myself is, "It's depression talking."

That's it, that's the secret: "It's depression talking."

It's amazing what a difference it can make simply to name your opponent. I learned this lesson early on, and forgot it. When I was maybe six years old, I had severe night terrors, as many bipolar children do. I was sure there was a beast living under my bed, just waiting for the dark so he could rip me apart and devour me for his dinner. I'd wake my poor parents in the middle of the night, sobbing and unable to be comforted.

Then one night my very wise father got down on his knees, looked under my bed, and said, "Is that who you're afraid of? Why, that's Ernie." Ernie, it seemed, was a jolly old monster who wanted nothing more than to watch over my dreams. It was hard to be afraid of a monster who had my best interests at heart. And nothing named Ernie can really be scary. I slept through the night after that.

I haven't quite evolved to the point where I can call my depression "Ernie." But I can call it by its rightful name, and recognize it when it comes too close, or tries to take up residence beneath my bed. Then I can do what needs to be done: call my doctor and adjust my meds; double up on therapy; stockpile comforting books and old movies; take great pains to eat and sleep well; and alert my closest friends. I can arm myself for battle.

"It's depression talking." That little phrase—and the world of knowledge that lies behind it—is the most powerful weapon I own.

— — —

HYPOMANIA

"That perfect bliss and sole felicity, the
sweet fruition of an earthly crown . . ."
—Christopher Marlowe (1564–1593),
Tamburlaine the Great

As the Harvard Medical School explains, "hypo" (from the Greek) means "under" or "less than." Hypomania therefore shares the same symptoms as mania, but they're less intense. It also lasts for a shorter duration, at least four consecutive days. The key difference between mania and hypomania, according to the DSM-5, is that a hypomanic episode isn't severe enough to cause marked impairment in social or occupational functioning, or to necessitate hospitalization, and there are no psychotic features.

So what's the problem necessitating a diagnosis? Hypomania can escalate into mania, or switch to serious depression. You can't always tell which one might happen because the pattern can be unpredictable. That's why some people—especially those with Bipolar II, who only experience hypomanic and depressive episodes—complain that it upsets the even rhythm of their lives. They may become very talkative, need less sleep, engage more socially, or otherwise feel and behave in ways that are different from their normal, everyday state. As the DSM-5 notes, this is often noticeable by others.

Dire consequences frequently result from mania's excesses and disregard for convention; in hypomania, not so much (https://www.healthline.com/health/mania-vs -hypomania#causes). There simply isn't the same clouding of judgment and itch to break the rules. And there can be significant rewards as well: a sublime sense of well-being, greater energy, enhanced creativity, and keener insight. If only it weren't for the Damocles's sword aspect to it—the perilous nature of so much happiness—perhaps people wouldn't complain at all.

THE PROZAC YEARS

It was the best relationship I've ever had. It lasted almost two years—two glorious years of waking up in the morning eager for the day to start, and falling asleep with a satisfied smile on my face. Two years of memory-making adventures, intense connection, and a harmony so complete it eludes description. The relationship wasn't with a man, or a woman, or even an animal. I was in love with myself.

I call them "the Prozac years." I hadn't yet been diagnosed with bipolar disorder. When I went to see a psychiatrist, all he witnessed was my crippling despair—the crying jags, the inability to move, the overwhelming wish to end it all. Not surprisingly, he diagnosed me with major depression. He was an excellent doctor, very up-to-the-minute, so it also wasn't a surprise that he prescribed Prozac, the latest wonder drug to hit the market.

It took a week or so to take effect, but oh my God, when it hit, it hit hard. It banished my depression to a faint if troubling memory. For the first time in ages, I actually looked forward to going to work—in fact, I almost craved the challenge. My mind had been lying dormant for so long, it was a thrill to be reintroduced to its abilities. I researched and wrote like a fiend, practically cackling with joy at the thought of whipping my adversaries. The partners in my law firm noticed and began giving me bigger and better cases, until my floor overflowed with files and I had to annex an adjoining office.

But it wasn't just in the law that I shone. My creativity, which I thought had all but disappeared, blossomed back to life and the old itch to write reasserted itself. So I took a writing class, joined a writing group, and rediscovered the bliss of putting just the right words in just the right order. I studied drawing and art history and English country gardens, and amassed a sizable collection of Sherlock Holmes apocrypha. That wasn't enough, though: I was fulfilling my own needs, but what about the world's? There were so many inequities staring me in the face, and I had the resources and energy to take them on. I sought out causes and represented them *pro bono*—one lawsuit went all the way up to the US Supreme Court. I finagled myself into an elite showbiz political coalition, and schmoozed my way to justice.

How did I take all of this on, while still billing such an extraordinary number of hours? I often look back at that time and wonder at its elasticity. It's as if my life expanded to meet my needs and my desires—and speaking of desire, I didn't skimp on socializing, either. I belonged to all the groups for up-and-coming professionals, and made the most of the opportunity to consort with anyone and everyone I found fascinating. And I found a great many people fascinating back then. The world was full of wonders, not all of them men.

Bad things naturally happened—I was, after all, performing for very high stakes in a high-stress environment, and I wasn't magically immune to sadness or disappointment. But they didn't burrow deep inside me and fester, as they used to. I didn't ruminate about them until all hours of the night. I told my doctor I felt like the beloved omelette pan I'd brought home from Paris. Somehow things didn't stick to me, they swooshed right off. I dealt with them and moved on.

I remember one Sunday afternoon hiking up to the Hollywood sign—yes, I even enjoyed hiking back then, such a stark contrast to the sedentary, practically paralyzed person I'd been when I was depressed. It was nearing the golden hour, when L.A. takes on a roseate glow that makes you believe in the divinity of beauty no matter how jaded you might be. I looked out over the city—my city—and made a mental note to remember that moment. Even now, I can still recall how happy and proud and grateful I felt. I was becoming the person I'd always wanted to be.

The Prozac years ended the following day.

I know because it was a Monday and I had a filing deadline in federal court—an answer to a complaint for copyright infringement that I'd already finished writing. All that was left to do was to get all the necessary copies made and send it by messenger to be filed and served. My secretary could handle most of that, I just had to stand by and make sure everything got done on time. But that morning, when the alarm clock rang, I felt the oddest lethargy. I hit the snooze button once, twice, then knocked the damn thing off the bedside table. It was past time for me to get in the shower, but the thought of that was repellent to me: all that water needling my skin.

When my eyes opened again, the sun was directly in them, which wasn't a good sign. I picked up the clock and swore: 1 p.m. I threw on a suit and gunned the Porsche and made it to the office in record time, only to find disaster waiting for me. The Xerox machines were down.

"They've been working on them all morning," my secretary told me, practically wringing her hands. "It's something electrical, they've called in an expert."

Normally I would have reassured her that it wasn't that big a deal, it would all turn out fine, and not to panic. Instead I marched into the copy room and corralled the head guy. "I've got a major filing due this afternoon, you have to fix it now," I said.

"We're working on it," he said. "But it seems—"

I raised my voice so all the copy guys could hear. "I don't want to hear but, I don't want to hear why. I want it fixed and I want it fixed now. Just do it, I don't care how." And I slammed the door behind me.

This wasn't like me at all—I'd always tried hard to maintain a good working relationship with the people who helped me. I needed them more than they needed me, and I knew it; I was careful with their feelings. But that day I was just plain furious and couldn't stop my anger from mounting. I yelled at my secretary to go stand in the copy room and watch, not that she could do anything but I was inexplicably mad at her, too.

The senior partner who was supervising the case stopped by my office. "What's happening with the filing?" he asked. I told him what was going on, and he lit into me the same way I had lit into the copy guys. "I already told the studio the answer was on its way," he said. "You've made me into a liar. Get it done, now."

When he left, I burst into tears even though I knew this was the way of the wolf pack I lived in: devour or be devoured. I felt helpless and hopeless, and the minutes just kept ticking by. I had to get the pleading out the door by 3 p.m. to beat the downtown traffic, and it was well past two o'clock. But my brain wouldn't work. It was thick and fuzzy, like a cloud of cotton wool. Beneath the fog lay something worse: a growing realization that I had changed, that things weren't swooshing off me anymore.

Purely out of the adrenaline of fear, I managed. I commandeered a Xerox machine from the bank downstairs, and hired a motorcycle messenger to weave in and out of the freeway traffic. The answer got filed on time—just barely. The crisis was averted, and I apologized to the copy guys and to my secretary for losing my cool. I apologized to the senior partner for making him sweat. But it didn't ease my heart one bit. I knew, by the time I finally got home, that something had been irretrievably lost that day—not the case, but my own serenity.

My doctor tried upping my Prozac dose, well past the recommended limit. But the drug had simply stopped working, just like that, and we never could figure out why. We tried adding on other antidepressants, antianxiety agents, antipsychotics. No response, only an ever-deepening return to the emotional abyss I'd known before—except when I got manic, which was its own spectacular kind of hell because my judgment became so severely impaired.

I did get hypomanic occasionally after that, but only for brief spurts, never for such an extended period of time. And the hypomania usually meant my mood was cycling, so there was a damper on my enjoyment of it. The omnipresent "Will it last?" spoiled some of the joy. Plus when I came down from those rarified heights, I was faced with the consequences of my success: the massive workload and the even more outsized expectations. But perhaps the most poignant pain of all was the loss of the identity I'd come to know and trust—and love so deeply.

There's an ache that is eternal in me, a longing for who I might be if only I were hypomanic again. It reminds me of my favorite lines in *The Tempest*, spoken by a tormented Caliban:

> *"Be not afeard; the isle is full of noises,*
> *Sounds, and sweet airs, that give delight*
> *   and hurt not . . .*
> *When I waked, I cried to dream again."*

— — —

SEDUCED BY A RIPE RED PLUM

Early this morning, without any warning at all, I woke up in the throes of euphoria. I threw off the covers, snapped on the light, and giggled from the sheer pleasure of being alive. What was I going to do with this frabjous day? Anything I wanted to. Everything I wanted to. I added a big dollop of cream to my coffee and devoured a blueberry scone dripping with honey. I indulged myself shamefully, without the shame.

But there was no time to waste: I was eager to be up and about and getting things done. Not monumental tasks, like saving the world, but essential ones, like getting groceries. There are no small parts, only small players, I reminded myself as I drove to my usual market. Halfway there, I pulled an illegal U-turn and headed back toward Gelson's. It was a Gelson's kind of day.

Let me describe: Gelson's is the *sine qua non* of supermarkets. When you walk in the door, it's like stepping into springtime. You're surrounded by orchids and lilies and swoons of roses, all begging to go home with you. There's a fountain somewhere, trickling water, and you don't even care if it's real or recorded. The cheese section alone is like a bucket-list journey to far-off places.

I gazed with longing at a tiny goat cheese labeled "Caprino di Foglia Noce," which sounded like a song sung by Venetian gondoliers at twilight.

"Would you care for a sample?" the cheese man said.

"Thank you, but I could never afford it," I replied.

"It is just for my pleasure," he said, cutting a slice and handing it to me on a napkin. He cut himself a slice, too. We looked into each other's eyes as the cheese melted into a moment.

Okay, not quite, but you get the drift. Gelson's is the place where food meets sex. On mornings like this when I'm so deeply attuned to my senses, I simply can't stay away. I know it's far beyond my budget, but what's money compared to a ripe red plum? Man made mere money; God made the plum.

I suppose I should have been somewhat concerned when I ate that red plum before paying for it. I'm not a thief, I never even shoplifted as a child; it's not my vice of choice. But it was an irresistible impulse, and usually I work hard at restraining those because they've gotten me into such trouble before. But somehow, that morning, I didn't even worry. It seemed perfectly natural to eat a plum in public, with the juices dribbling down my chin.

The produce man appeared at my side. I thought he was going to haul me in for questioning, but instead he said, "The pluots are even better, Miss. Here, try one." I started to decline, but his smile was so eager and the "Miss" so charming I had to accept. He called over his shoulder, "Enrique, bring a napkin," and in an instant a young man was at my elbow. A young man, did I say? More like a Nijinsky fawn.

He looked familiar, and I had to wonder: Had I slept with him before? There was a certain knowingness about his smile . . . and it was a real possibility. This town is littered with intimate manic encounters I don't remember at all. Embarrassed, I took the napkin and spoke to my shoes. "Thank you," I said. "Delicious." I grabbed some pluots and wheeled my cart toward the checkout counter. It was high time I left heaven.

I showed the checker the plum pit, confessed my sin, and told her to charge me whatever she liked.

"Oh, people do that all the time," she said. "But you're the first one who's ever offered to pay."

"That's shocking," I said.

"Well, it's nice to know there's at least one honest person left," she said. She rang up my other items, and I waited for her to assess my penalty.

"Get along with you now," she said.

I smiled. She smiled. The boy bagging my groceries smiled. The whole world was one big greeting card.

Damn. Damn. And damn again.

I knew it must be hypomania because life just ain't this grand. Hypomania is that exquisite state one rung below mania, where I feel like I can conquer the world—but I don't try to because some vestige of reality still exists in my brain. I'm not wildly reckless or grandiose, as in mania. Just friendly as hell and thrilled to be wherever I am. I can barely remember what depression felt like, it seems so distant and foreign to my nature.

And what's really great is, everyone likes me. It must be some kind of pheromone or happiness hormone that I unconsciously transmit in this state. Or maybe it's my genuine joy that draws people toward me and encourages them to be joyful back. I don't know, I'm not a connoisseur of charismatic phenomena. But I swear this really happens: it's impossible for me not to seduce the universe when I'm hypomanic.

Sounds delicious, doesn't it? It is. It's the single most splendid feeling on earth, a divine reward for all the torment I otherwise have to endure with bipolar disorder. So why do I curse it? Because like all things perfect and ephemeral—a first kiss, that first wolfish bite of plum—hypomania doesn't last forever. Those few brief days of bliss are a signal that I'm cycling again. That no matter how good I may feel at the moment, I'm about to morph into a totally different mood state, one with none of the glory and all of the risk. There's no real certainty when this will happen, or in which direction I'll go. There's only the waiting . . .

Oh come on, I thought, as I waited for the Gelson's valet to bring me my car. Life has handed me a plum. Can't I just enjoy it while it lasts? Do I have to be so hypervigilant, always slapping a price tag on something that feels so organic, so right? In short, why can't this be my new normal? That's easy. Because I'm not, and never have been, "normal." But I do get to be utterly glorious, every once in a while.

— — —

WHERE THE NEON LIGHTS ARE PRETTY

I had an argument with an old boyfriend on our way to a party. I was in a really good mood and couldn't stop talking about it. "I mean, I feel *really* good, you know? Like end-of-the-school-term, beginning-of-summertime good. Do you think that's okay?"

"Why wouldn't it be?" he said.

"I don't want to be inappropriate."

"It's a party, for God's sake, not a funeral," he said. "Everyone's supposed to be happy."

"But do I seem all right? If you just met me, would you think I was acting okay?"

"You live in such a threat-based universe," he scowled. "I swear, even when you're happy you're waiting to see how it's going to end."

I rolled down the window and stuck my head out to enjoy the breeze, like a besotted cocker spaniel. Maybe my friend was right, but he didn't know why. The truth is, I've had to think very hard about happiness: its beginnings and its inevitable endings, too. Whenever I start to feel this good, I have to wonder: *Is this what other people experience? Am I merely hypomanic? Or am I too, too happy for words and maybe trembling on the brink of mania? What's the proper happiness quotient under any given circumstance?* I don't want to exceed it, but I want my fair share, too.

I stuck my head back in the car and turned on the oldies station. The Monkees were singing "I'm a Believer." Joy and bliss! I sang along as loudly as I could until my friend snapped the radio off.

"Okay, maybe now you're a bit overmuch," he said.

"Thanks, sweetie," I said. "I appreciate your concern." I smiled at him as if he'd just given me an Hermès scarf. Then I turned the radio back on, full blast. "Sugar, Sugar," sang the Archies.

"You've got to be kidding," he said, and turned the volume way down. I pouted and put my head out the window again. But I didn't stay miffed for long; I couldn't. I was in that rare place of unreachability, where nothing miserly or nasty or icky can touch me. Aaaah, the light. Mmm, the breeze. And ohhh, what it was doing to my hair. A thousand tingly caresses from root to tip, sending quivers of pleasure down my spine. Such an amazingly beautiful day! I stretched my arms out the window, trying to grasp handfuls of sunshine.

My friend looked over. "Terri, what are you doing?" He reeled me in by the back of my dress.

"Thanks, sweetie," I said, unruffled except for my hair. "I appreciate your concern." I smiled at him as if he'd just given me ruby slippers.

That's the problem with happiness, I thought: It always makes us want more, and more is always out there, just out of reach. Hence addiction. Hence obsession. Would we suffer these maladies of desire if we hadn't known that initial thrill of pleasure? I doubted it.

"Happiness is a gateway drug," I announced to my friend.

He glanced over at me and cocked an eyebrow. "Where'd you get that—from a bumper sticker?"

"No, it's an epiphany all my own. Do you like it?"

"I'm driving," he said. So I turned the radio back up.

Petula Clark came on, singing one of my all-time favorites, "Downtown." It was absolute perfection, every word matching my mood as she raved on about the traffic and the music and the neon signs, so pretty . . . Downtown sounded like the apotheosis of everything I was longing for: liberation, blazing excitement, endless possibilities for pleasure. I started dancing as best I could in the confines of the car—snapping my fingers and bouncing to the irresistible beat. The pressure inside me was building and bubbling and I couldn't resist it any longer.

I sank back in my seat and allowed happiness to flood me, a pure unadulterated whoosh of joy. Uh-oh. That worry again: Was I getting manic? I didn't think so. I looked over at my ex and realized I didn't have the slightest desire to seduce him because he was being such a jerk. So okay, my judgment was still intact. I relaxed my vigilance and let my neurons explode.

Connections, connections, everywhere—like an arcade game playing inside my head. Ping, pong, whoosh, zap. Connections were falling into place, huge rents in the fabric of existence suddenly visible. Colors collided, shadows burst into light. It was thrilling but also a little scary, and I wondered, *is it safe*? Maybe I ought to shut my eyes; maybe such sights weren't mine to see. But I wanted it all, I wanted more, more, more.

"Come on, baby," I said. "Let's go downtown."

— — —

MIXED STATE

"The discontented man finds no easy chair."
—Benjamin Franklin (1706–1790)

▬ ▬ ▬

Although around 40 percent of people with bipolar disorder will experience a "mixed state" during their lifetimes, according to a University of Siena School of Medicine study, it's a mystery even to health care professionals. It's so difficult to describe even they can't agree on a good name for it, let alone a consensual definition. I've heard it called "agitated depression." "Dysphoric mania." "Episode with mixed features."

The problem starts with the terms "bipolar" and its predecessor, "manic depression," which make it sound like there are only two emotional poles to the illness: mania and depression. Actually, it's possible to experience elements of *both* these states at one time, simultaneously or in rapid sequence. For example, you can feel extremely agitated and restless, as in mania, but also deeply disgusted with yourself and life, as in depression.

It's a very dangerous combination because you have the energy to act on your destructive instincts—unlike in pure depression, where you're usually too paralyzed to act or plan. In fact, as the *Scientific World Journal* confirmed, the majority of suicides are committed during mixed states. So call it what you like, one thing is certain: it's the mood state that I dread the most.

— — —

THE TORPEDO RED BLUES

Extreme irritability is apparently becoming part of my identity, the new hallmark of my bipolar disorder. It usually happens in mixed state episodes, that frenetic combination of mania and depression that I seem to be experiencing more and more frequently these days. It's taken me years to realize that I'm not just incredibly cranky, I'm cycling. The reason my discovery was delayed so long is that, like everything else with bipolar disorder, a clear pattern had to emerge. That's why it so often takes people ten years to get a correct diagnosis of this illness: one needs time to discern a landscape of shifting moods.

So one particularly annoying day, I ventured out seeking distraction—anything to get me out of my twitchy mind and itchy skin. I decided to return a lipstick I'd mistakenly bought. When I'd opened the box, I realized it wasn't my favorite Torpedo Red bullet. It was something called "Pink Lotus," and pink anything sounded vile to me. The store's parking lot was packed to the gills, but I spotted an elderly woman coming out of the elevator and practically hit her with my bumper as I stalked her to her car. I wanted to roll down my window and shout, "Can't you walk any faster?" but I sat in my car, inched forward, and fumed.

The saleswoman at the makeup counter was wearing way too much perfume, even if it was the brand's signature scent. And too much makeup—was she a walking advertisement for the entire line? But no one else was available, so I let her live. I handed her the lipstick.

"This is the wrong shade," I said. "I want to return it."

"Do you have the receipt?" she said. Right, like I save every teeny-tiny piece of paper that happens to come my way.

"I threw it out," I said.

"Without a receipt, I'm afraid there's nothing we can do," she said.

"Then I'll take a store credit."

"But this box has been opened," she said. "We can't take back used cosmetics. It's simply a matter of hygiene, you see."

A snarl was climbing up my spine. I forced it down. "But I didn't use the lipstick itself," I said. I grabbed it back from her and snapped off the cover. "Look, it's completely intact."

"I'm afraid that's our store policy," she said. "Once an item is opened, it can't be returned."

"But I did not open the lipstick. What about that do you not understand?" *Uh-oh*, I thought, *I'm dropping my contractions.* When my language starts sounding all formal and stilted, it means I'm pushing the limits of my self-control.

Her plumped lips pouted sweetly, as she shook her head. "I'm sorry, it's really out of my hands."

"Then whose hands is it in, may I ask?"

"I'll have to get my manager," she said, and a few minutes later an even more doll-like face appeared, half my age and probably half my IQ. I explained the situation slowly to her, enunciating each syllable so she could understand. Then I waived the pristine tube in front of her face. "You see? Never used."

"Yes, but you opened the box," she said.

"But I did not open the lipstick."

"Yes, but you opened the box."

As a rule, I try to govern my emotions in public, which isn't easy because my emotions don't like to be governed. But it's the price of mental illness: One must preserve the appearance of propriety at all times. It's very important for those of us who roil on the inside to present as smooth and unruffled on the outside. Otherwise, what might happen? Censure, certainly. A scene? Inevitably. I knew all this. I knew I should just walk away. And I knew that was never going to happen.

I opened the tube and dialed out the lipstick. I smiled. Then in one fluid motion, I scrawled "F**K" across the countertop. "Now you're right," I said. "It's been used." I dropped the tube and walked—no, strode—out of the store.

Did it make me feel better? Hell yes, for a minute or two. But when I tried to get my car keys out of my purse, I realized I was shaking. Not just trembling from adrenaline—shaking with fear. I'd violated my own social compact: I'd lost control in public. Maybe other people can get away with being miffed and acting out. Hey, we all have our Pink Lotus moments. But I can't afford them. My moods don't just ignite and die down, they detonate—usually in front of people who can do me harm: security guards, police officers, and other authority figures who tease my temper beyond all bounds.

I tried to cool down. "It's just a mixed state," I told myself. But I knew better: There's no "just" when it comes to a mixed state. There's only trouble ahead.

My hands were still shaking when I fished out my phone and speed-dialed my psychiatrist. "It's starting," I told his voicemail. "Oh God, it's starting again." I knew I didn't have to tell him what "it" was, he'd seen me like this too often before. And I knew exactly what he'd do: call in a prescription for lithium, the pale pink dial-down drug. That would put any chance I might have of illicit joy and madness effectively out of my reach. I'd be slow and cautious and seemingly calm, and I wouldn't make a fuss over anything because nothing would really matter. But it wouldn't last. It never does. I knew she'd be back—the Torpedo Red woman—once I cared enough about life to be irritable again.

— — —

BIPOLAR DISORDER'S NASTY SECRET

It was a gorgeous day, the kind Southern California is famous for. Maybe too gorgeous: the birds trilling outside my window harped on my nerves, the abundant sunshine made me squint. The telephone rang and I barked, "What is it?" instead of hello. I got rid of the caller as quickly as possible and fixed myself a cup of coffee. But the mug was too hot and it singed my fingers. I threw it in the sink, where it shattered into dozens of tiny pieces.

It was my favorite mug, not just because of its hand-painted sunflowers but because it was the last remaining souvenir of a weekend tryst with a long-lost lover. There would never be another mug like that, or another man like him, or another love affair worth remembering. My life was as good as over. Carelessly, my eyesight blurred by tears, I tried to sweep up the shards in the sink; but they cut me and I started to bleed. I picked up one of the larger slivers and deliberately sliced my finger—my oh-so-naked ring finger, a glaring reminder of my failure at love. More blood, merging with the rest and coursing down the drain. How quickly here and forgotten, like me.

All that afternoon, I continued to swirl between emotions, not a single good one in the bunch. Misery, fear, self-loathing—all the classic notes of depression were there, but they were overlaid with the least desirable aspects of mania. No euphoria, no elation, none of that sky-high, soaring giddiness that makes a manic mood worthwhile. Just a relentless, pulsing energy that seized hold of my body and urged it to move, move, move. But move where? Move why? My mind insisted I had no viable destination.

I kept thinking about my old boyfriend and that last weekend we had spent together at San Ysidro, so in love, so eager to be together. Then, too, it had dawned a beautiful day, but I'd woken up snappish, on edge for no reason. I'd never heard of a "mixed state" back then. I didn't know that when mania and depression collide, it creates a whole new realm of madness. Not many people know this is part of the bipolar spectrum; I certainly didn't. All I knew then was that the world would be wise not to get in my way.

My poor boyfriend tried all the wrong approaches. First, he tried to nuzzle me, but I was too prickly to be touched. Then he tried logic: it was a lovely day, we were together, there was nothing to be upset about. Big mistake. I was still practicing law at that time, and I out-argued him with ease. He got furious, as men frequently do when you best them. But his anger was no match for me. I could feel words climbing up my throat—you know those words that you absolutely have to keep suppressed at all times? Every relationship has them. There are certain things you can never say, certain weaknesses you're not allowed to exploit, unless you're willing to suffer the consequences.

I didn't care. I spewed them at him, vile words that I won't even repeat because I wish them to vanish forever. He was gone before my tears reached my cheeks.

Mixed states are all about smashing up things: mugs, relationships, best intentions. I realize that now, and it makes me careful. Whenever I find myself in the cyclone's path, I don't go out. I limit my interactions with people as much as possible, to prevent them—and myself—from getting hurt. I know that the mixed state is stronger than I am, but that doesn't mean it has to own me, body and soul. I may cut a finger; I may break some glass. But now that I know what I'm up against, I refuse—when I can—to get swept away.

— — —

RAPID CYCLING

"Life is measured by the rapidity of change . . ."
—George Eliot (1819–1880)

— — —

Change is a constant with bipolar disorder—but constant change is not. Rapid cycling is a phenomenon in which the course of the illness is accelerated: at least four mood episodes in the previous twelve months that meet the criteria for mania, hypomania, or major depression. In extreme cases, one can go through multiple moods in a single day. This is called "ultraradian rapid cycling"—a rather lovely phrase for a very distressing condition.

A review of the scientific literature by the *Journal of Clinical Psychiatry* found that rapid cycling affects at least a quarter of bipolar patients and is related to a longer course of illness, an earlier age at onset, and more illegal drug and alcohol use. Its cause remains unclear, although hypothyroidism may be implicated. Ironically, the use of antidepressants, which are frequently prescribed, can trigger or worsen cycling.

Understandably, doctors find rapid cycling very hard to manage because symptoms slip away before they can be properly treated, only to be replaced by new ones. Loved ones find it confusing and even infuriating because they don't know which person will show up when, and this unpredictability may be construed as intentional or indulgent. I've been a rapid cycler all my life, and even I can't keep up with my moods. But it has one advantage: although I don't know how I'll feel on any given occasion, I know I won't feel that way forever.

— — —

THORNS TODAY, ROSES TOMORROW

Even I had to admit I was acting weird the week before my birthday: elated one minute, dejected the next, my emotions flitting too quickly through me to be properly felt and acknowledged. Since mood lability is the premier symptom of my bipolar disorder, I wondered, briefly, if I should call my doctor to adjust my meds. But I just chalked it up to birthday nerves. Everybody gets them, right?

I never like to admit that I'm symptomatic. It makes me feel weak and deficient. *If only I were stronger*, I think, *I could just master my mind and be done with it.* None of this up and down, hither and thither, all-over-the-place emoting. The fact that there's a clinical name for such extreme volatility—rapid cycling—doesn't make it any more palatable. My feelings can fluctuate more quickly than a twitchy stock market. It's exhausting to be catapulted around this way.

But the morning of my birthday I woke up feeling just fine. Delicious, in fact. My cheeks were slightly flushed and my eyes extra bright. I was looking forward to the birthday lunch my girlfriends had scheduled at a lovely restaurant in Brentwood. I arrived extra early to pick out our table: a cozy nook under a canopy of flowering vines that would perfectly frame my face. When you're bipolar and always trying to hide your symptoms, you think a lot about self-presentation.

The minute my friends arrived, I started to talk—about anything and everything and nothing, and why not? It was my birthday, and I had the floor. The topic soon turned to travel, and I offered up my adventures on safari in Kenya in considerable detail. I suspected I was talking way too much when my friends stopped asking questions and simply stared at me. Mania just loves to hear itself talk.

But I wasn't manic, I told myself. I was naturally exuberant because it was my birthday. And to prove it, I forced myself to speak more slowly and ask my friends about their own travels. It was incredibly hard, like wrestling a kite down out of the sky in a storm, but I did it. See? Not manic.

My friends countered with their own stories, of India and Kyoto and Cairo and Bali. And China. And Thailand. And Tibet. By the time the comparative merits of Himalayan spas had entered the conversation, I found I'd run out of things to contribute. I grew quieter and quieter, feeling ever more out of place and provincial. There's nothing worse than being forlorn among friends.

By then the sun had shifted, and the foliage was casting a shadow across our table. I was suddenly tired, so tired I could barely say my good-byes. Driving home, I started crying so hard my tears blinded me and I nearly had an accident. *I should never socialize*, I thought. It always ends badly. Nobody really likes me, anyway— why force my company on them?

When I opened my gate, I stumbled over a long cardboard box. Yellow roses, two dozen of them. From the right guy. As I arranged them in my favorite vase, I started to hum. Softly at first, then what the hell—I belted it out like Liza: "Life is a cabaret, old chum! Come to the cabaret . . ."

A thorn pricked my finger, and I went into the bathroom to wash off the blood. My reflection made no sense to me: my eyes were luminous, lit up by my smile, but they were shrouded by long black streaks of mascara. It was a most undeniably bipolar face. For a moment, I thought again of calling my doctor. But I went back into the kitchen instead and inhaled my yellow roses. There was plenty of time, after all. I'd still be bipolar tomorrow, and who knew how I'd feel by then?

— — —

THE WORLD'S WORST PARTY GUEST

A while back, I had to go off some of my meds, and I found myself at the mercy of my moods—a very slippery place to be. I can go up and down and over and sideways with scarcely a heartbeat in between. This rapid cycling poses a genuine problem when I'm expected to act like a rational, ordinary human being: for example, a gracious guest. A recent overnight stay at a friend's house got me thinking about all the possible do's and don'ts in this situation. I may exaggerate a little—but alas, only a little.

DO'S AND DON'TS:

1. Accept the invitation with delight when you're manic and volunteer to bring your famous chicken cacciatore as the main course for twelve people.
2. When the day of the party arrives, be wretchedly depressed and get greasy Chinese takeout instead.
3. Show up morose and forget everyone's names, especially those people you've known forever.
4. Have a glass of wine at dinner even though your doctors forbid it because it destabilizes you. Have two. Get manic.
5. Deliver a scintillating monologue on politics and religion. Do not pause for breath to allow others to express their opinions.
6. Regale the table with a graphic account of your experience with electroshock therapy because it is, after all, your mission in life to educate the uninformed.
7. Refuse to listen to any questions because it is not, after all, your responsibility in life to mollycoddle the ignorant.
8. Contradict yourself frequently and when called on it, quote Walt Whitman: "Do I contradict myself? Very well then, I contradict myself." Revel in the ensuing silence.

9. When guests start to leave, hug and kiss them inappropriately, especially those you barely know. Slip them your card and suggest you get together soon with a knowing wink.

10. When your host says it's time to turn in, ask for a big glass of water and take a whopping handful of pills in front of him. This will undoubtedly reassure him that you're not going to burn down the house while he sleeps.

11. Screw up and take your morning meds instead of your evening ones, so you're wired to the gills.

12. Wander the house at night while everyone else is asleep. Tiptoe into the other bedrooms and sneak a peek at people while they're sleeping and at their most vulnerable.

13. Open up the pantry and take out all the food so you can rearrange it in alphabetical order. Your host will thank you when he finds out.

14. Get bored halfway through and abandon the project at "Jasmine tea."

15. Go into the bathroom and stare at yourself for twenty minutes. Feel intensely lonely because you're the only one up, staring at herself in bad lighting. Get maudlin and start to cry.

16. Sit down on the toilet and cry until your eyes are swollen and you've used up all the toilet paper.

17. Decide to leave before anyone can see you looking so hideous. Pack up your things and sneak out the front door.

18. Set off the alarm. Do not, on any account, come back to explain.

19. Five days later, when you're hypomanic, send your host a huge bouquet of dahlias and a witty thank-you note.

20. Do not expect a reply.

— — —

SUICIDALITY

"Death is defiance."
—Virginia Woolf (1882–1941),
Mrs. Dalloway

Our country is facing an unprecedented suicide epidemic. According to a shocking 2018 study by the Centers for Disease Control (CDC), the national suicide rate is the highest it has been in fifty years. It increased by more than 33 percent just since 1999. Every day, 121 more Americans will die by their own hands. What accounts for this tragedy?

It used to be a commonplace theory that over 90 percent of those who died by suicide suffered from a mental illness. But as the rate skyrockets, traditional thinking is changing. We are only beginning to realize the complexities of suicide—that it is a multidimensional issue, and that "mental illness" is a much broader concept than was previously thought. Substance abuse (particularly opioids), income inequality, the mechanization of the economy, relationship conflicts, the ready availability of guns, sexual trauma, marginalization—all of these social stressors and more potentially give rise to suicidal thoughts and attempts.

Now, the CDC reports that about half—54 percent—of people who died by suicide did **not** have a known mental illness. The American Psychiatric Association rightly asserts that many of these people may have been dealing with mental health challenges that had not yet been diagnosed or known to those around them. This is terrifying, and the challenge is clear: to prevent suicide, we must identify concerns earlier and more thoroughly.

A friend of mine, a suicide expert, calls this "upstreaming." It's particularly compelling since the rate of teenage suicide is through the roof, the highest it has been since the US government began collecting statistical data in 1960. This year, 16 percent of adolescents will consider killing themselves—and suicide is the second leading cause of death in the ten-to-twenty-four-year-old demographic.

The Harvard Medical School agrees that we need to adopt "a lifelong prevention approach of detecting psychological distress and trauma exposure at onset." It believes this could provide America "with a resilience platform for averting [this] epidemic." The utmost vigilance is clearly required—suicide is a harrowing ordeal that no one should ever be tempted near, lest, God forbid, they wind up another statistic.

— — —

THE END, AND THEN

Many years ago, on a cold winter's trip, I tried to kill myself by over-dosing on pills. It was a calm, deliberate, self-willed act. The original reason for my attempt—my beloved father's painful death from cancer—had been eclipsed by a raging chemical depression from which I was sure I would never recover. So I figured I was free to end my life if I wanted to because there was no conceivable future left for me. But events beyond my control intervened and to my horror and shame, I continued to live.

Not long after I was discharged from the hospital, I walked out one night in the falling snow. It was dark and eerily quiet. I walked for thirty minutes or so, not caring where I was going. Exhausted, I stopped in a deserted park, unable to take another step. My father was gone, and all my best-laid plans to end my life had failed. So what was the point of going forward? And I didn't just mean walking on in the snow.

I was too tired to wait for an answer, and too cold to listen for one. All I wanted to do was sleep and sleep and sleep. I lay down on the soft fluffy pillow of snow and closed my eyes. *You're going to freeze to death,* I thought, *but at least this was a pleasant way to go.* It couldn't hurt for very long . . . but it did. My arms and legs began to ache, and instinct took over. I furiously waved them up and down to get my circulation going. When the blood finally started to flow again, I got back on my feet and looked around for a clue to tell me where I was. But I didn't see any landmarks or street signs. What I saw was that I'd made angel wings in the snow.

Since my botched overdose a few weeks before, I'd tried hard to stop my brain from thinking. But there, in the absolute quiet, I could hear it coming alive again; its constant refrain was, why? I'd plotted and planned; I'd acted with malice aforethought. I didn't care if I was committing a crime against nature—so be it. We all have the right to do wrong. But in spite of my strenuous effort, I'd been syringed and pumped and shocked back to life. Why, a thousand times, why? Why this particular ending instead?

I didn't want to believe it, but the evidence was pretty hard to ignore: Maybe the right to die wasn't mine after all. Maybe there were things left to do, words left to speak, that were beyond my comprehension. Was it possible life wanted more from me, and I had more to give? There in the freezing cold, I took an honest inventory of myself. There was only one thing I knew I could do, but it was important: I could bear witness to the pain of depression.

Depression was real.

Depression was physical.

Depression wanted you dead.

I swore right then and there that I wouldn't stop calling depression out. I wouldn't let anyone forget what a monstrosity, a miscreant, an abomination it was—the antithesis of all that was clean and whole. And I wouldn't stop exposing suicide as the great untruth, the lie masquerading as a promise.

My attempt had shocked me into sharper focus, and made me realize my own tensile strength. I knew then that I had the ability to fall from grace, and to get back up and keep on moving. Maybe I'd survived because this was where I needed to be: shivering but alive to tell the tale. Maybe it was as simple as that. I had to remember this moment, and I had to share it. I'd been as low as a person could possibly get, and yet—I'd made angel wings in the snow.

I DIDN'T PLAN TO GO TO THE ER THAT NIGHT . . .

I woke up in a sweat, confused and disoriented, as if I'd just emerged from a too-vivid dream. I went to the bathroom to run a cool wash-cloth over my face. At least, I think that's what happened. All I really know for sure (and I'm not too clear about this) is that I fell and fell hard, hitting my head and my side on the edge of the bathtub. I know this from the contusions that are starting to erupt, and from the ongoing pain in my head. But that night, when I came to, all I thought was: *This is it. I'm going to die.*

I didn't think this because I'd had a bad fall. I thought it because I was unable to move. I laid my head down on the bathroom rug and passed out. Again and again I tried to get up, only to lose consciousness. I realized in those few brief moments of wakefulness that I needed to call 911. But the phone was in my bedroom, which seemed a thousand feet away. My only possible hope was to drag myself over there in between swoons.

Time swirled—it felt like hours—but I finally made it across the room and dialed. The operator answered right away, and all I could say was "I fell" before I became unconscious again, dropping the phone on the floor. To my everlasting astonishment and grat-itude, the 911 operator was able to trace my call, and shortly after that the ambulance arrived.

The siren woke me, and I heard voices shouting that they were going to have to break down the door. Dying or not, I knew my landlord would kill me, so I managed to crawl over and unlock it. When the paramedics entered, the first thing they must have seen were my drugs. There are bottles of them scattered all over the place, and an even greater cornucopia spilling out of my kitchen drawers.

"Did you try to commit suicide, ma'am?" one of the paramedics asked me. Then he slapped me awake and I shook my head no.

"What are all these drugs?" he said.

"Drugs," I answered, as if that were obvious.

"What are you taking them for?"

"Bipolar—" I said, before I passed out. I don't remember anything else, just waking up in a hospital bed at Cedars-Sinai and knowing I must have screwed up somehow. I don't usually end up in the emergency room unless it's at the other end of an overdose.

Something must have gone wrong with my drugs. Whenever really bad things happen to me, it always has something to do with my drugs. I must have inadvertently taken my night medications twice, was all I could think, because they are super-sedating and would explain my incoherence and inability to stay awake. This was a very likely possibility, but I couldn't communicate it to anyone. Words were like butterflies flitting around my head, and I had no net to catch them.

I heard a voice above me say, "Probable suicide attempt."

"No!" I wanted to shout, but my thick slab of tongue got in the way.

"Do an ethylene alcohol lab," someone else said, and then I got angry because I've been sober for ages. But the butterflies swarmed and my head hit the pillow, and once again, I knew no more.

When I woke, I was consumed by regret. My splendid record of no suicide attempts for at least ten years was going to be demolished, simply because I couldn't speak. I kept trying to signal a nurse for something to write on, but just try getting ahold of an ER nurse. It's like trying to tackle a Green Bay Packer. Now I was the one slapping my face, to keep awake so I could somehow explain my situation. That was more important to me than finding out what damage I'd done to my body.

I finally managed to croak a few words, and then I knew I was going to live; because as long as I have words at my disposal, I have a semblance of power over my fate. I snagged a passing white coat. "I didn't try—" was all I could get out, before he shook off my hand and went on his way. But with the next white coat I got luckier. "I didn't try to kill myself," I said, halting between words for emphasis.

"Let's have a look at your code," he said, pulling a slim chart from the foot of my bed. "Hmm—a 99285."

"Huh?"

"That means a significant threat to life or function, requiring advanced life support. It also says here that you're bipolar and attempted suicide."

I wanted to scream but I realized that was unlikely to help my case. "Absolutely not," I whispered, pulling him down by his sleeve so he could hear me better. "I didn't. I swear. You've got to change the chart."

"Are you sure?" he asked. "Because it looks pretty bad, all those drugs lying around and you unresponsive."

"I'm positive. Please," I begged him, then I thought of the ultimate tactic, the clincher. "I'm a lawyer," I said, as loudly as I could. As I knew it would, that worked. Saying I'm a lawyer almost always gets me out of trouble; I don't know why. Perhaps the doctor was afraid of liability, or he was suddenly convinced of my credibility. Whatever. I was willing to don my dreaded J.D. again if it would clear my name.

Maybe you have to be a survivor of multiple suicide attempts to understand how urgent this felt. I was so proud of my "clean and sane" time—the many, many occasions when I'd wanted to kill myself but had resisted the temptation. It had been so hard when I was suffering to put all the pills back into their bottles, to log off the creepy instructional websites, undo the nooses I'd so carefully tied, and commit to yet another day. Sometimes it had taken every last ounce of my will and every last vestige of prayer, but somehow I had done it for ten whole years and no one—no one!—was going to snatch that accomplishment away from me.

I'm beginning now to receive what I'm sure will be dozens of exorbitant medical bills. But they can't overshadow the joy of the final verdict, which is printed proof on those bills: "Overdose, accidental/unintentional." In all my years of practicing law, it's my sweetest victory. It's proof that I've chosen to live.

NEVER BE FOOLED BY A SMILE

It was just another day. I was driving to the car wash when I got an email from a friend back east. The subject line was oddly worded, and for a few moments its true meaning didn't sink in. "My Wife Rebecca Taking Her Own Life," it said. It sounded like it was describing a picture or a video, and I couldn't even begin to imagine what that would look like. But the body of the email went on to explain that my friend's wife, Rebecca, had died by suicide. The message didn't offer any explanations, only details of a memorial service to be held in a few days.

I pulled over to the side of the road and waited for a reaction to flood me. But all I could feel was surprise. Surely there was a mistake, the message wasn't meant for me, it was some other Rebecca, somebody else's tragedy. The Rebecca I knew would never have taken her own life. Sure, she had a mental illness and suffered greatly from it at times. But she would never have given up the fight.

I'd met Rebecca and her then-boyfriend Frank at a mental health support group in L.A. Frank was bipolar, and I believe Rebecca's last diagnosis was schizoaffective. I wasn't all that fond of the group, but I was very fond of Rebecca and Frank. They made such a charming couple—both struggling but very supportive of each other. And they were so knowledgeable about their conditions. They read everything, attended every local lecture on the subject, and could pass for doctors if one didn't know better.

It's true that Rebecca was sometimes slightly "off"—I could tell her medications weren't working quite right at those times. She would stare into space or answer a question a few beats too slowly. But that was just a small blip on the screen; the big picture was so impressive. Rebecca had graduated UCLA with a psychology major and attained her master's degree in another field. She knew where she was going: she wanted to teach, and I always thought her future students would be lucky to have her.

I ran into Frank a few years later, and he told me that he and Rebecca were going to be married. They were planning to live in Iowa, and attend school there so Rebecca could get yet another degree. I was sorry to see them go, but so proud of them for achieving the American dream, in spite of the significant odds against them. They were a true success story—proof to many of us with mental illness that love and marriage were not impossible goals.

She did everything right. What could have possibly gone so wrong?

Recently Frank got back in touch with me. He sent me a picture of Rebecca, taken shortly before she killed herself. You can't imagine a sweeter scene: Rebecca curled up on a couch with her beloved cat, a beatific smile on her face. If angels ever deign to live on earth, that's what Rebecca looked like. What in God's name had happened?

Frank told me he blamed himself for Rebecca's suicide, which troubled me because he always took such good care of her. He had been called out of town, he said, and she was lonely and anxious without him. He felt like he hadn't been paying close enough attention, and didn't take her expressions of pain seriously enough. As he so poignantly put it, "I didn't understand her intent until I learned she was dead."

I tried to reassure him that suicide often has very little to do with the people around you. It's an intensely personal act; the emotional pain blots out any thoughts you might have about how your actions could affect others. Too often, there's no obvious warning. And afterward no good answer to the endless "why." Then I emailed the picture of Rebecca to people who were close to me. "Just so you know," I wrote. "You have to watch for suicide, like you'd watch a smoldering fire."

I wonder how many people really understood what I meant. I got responses like, "What a pretty girl" and "What a beautiful picture." They wanted to know if the cat was all right. But no one responded directly to my warning about suicide. I guess the world is too willing to be fooled by a smile.

Take it from someone who's been there and back: If you love a person who's suicidal, you have to see beyond that smile. It's all too easy to look fine and feel desperate. In my own life, the closer I've come to killing myself, the finer I've appeared. I don't want to be foiled at the last minute, so I pretend I'm getting better. Maybe I even look like Rebecca on that couch.

But you have to ask, and keep on asking those people in pain: Do you have a plan, are you stockpiling pills, is there a gun in the house? Sure, they may get annoyed with you, but annoyed is better than dead. Do I wish my loved ones had nagged me like this, and seen past my facade? Yes. Do I blame them? No. As I told Frank, suicide is nobody else's fault—it's your life to live, and yours to end.

And yet . . . For all my cool, dispassionate take on the subject, the truth is I'm still terrified by how close I've come to dying. A child's voice inside me says, why weren't they watching more closely? Why did they leave me alone? Of course, as a grown-up, I realize how utterly unrealistic this is. No one has X-ray vision; Superman's just a cartoon. But you get very small when you're suicidal. You want to be looked after, coddled, taken by the hand to cross the street. Part of you really wants to be watched, even as you push people away.

Rebecca, if you're listening, I promise you: my eyes are wide open now.

THE MIND-BODY CONNECTION

"A sick thought can devour the body's flesh
more than fever or consumption."
—Guy de Maupassant (1850–1893),
Le Horla et Autres Contes Fantastiques

Whoever came up with the term "mental illness"? I'd like to meet him and smack him around. He did us a grave disservice because what we deem mental illness isn't just limited to the brain. According to the National Institutes of Health, "there is no real division between mind and body because of networks of communication that exist between the brain and neurological, endocrine and immune systems." An increasing number of medical schools, including Harvard, UCLA, and Columbia, now have departments devoted to mind-body research and treatment.

This relatively new interdisciplinary field, often called psychoneuroimmunology, has witnessed an explosion of empirical findings. Among the most promising theories being tested is that mental illness may have its root in inflammation, the by-product of an overactive immune system (https://www .health.harvard.edu/newsletter_article/infection-inflammation -and-mental-illness). The discovery of objective "proof" of mental illness—that elusive biomarker that would verify a diagnosis— could have profound results on treatment. Just as importantly, it could greatly diminish both societal and self-imposed stigma by facilitating "a shift toward parity of esteem between physical and mental health" (https://www.ncbi.nlm.nih.gov/pmc /articles/PMC5436791/).

The science may sound complicated, but the conclusion is simple: Mind and body aren't strangers who haven't been introduced. What affects one is very likely to affect the other. Maybe we find that frightening because it dissolves our artificial limits. It shows that mental illness is systemic and consumes far more territory than we had previously believed. In short, the mind leaks.

WHEN YOUR MIND WON'T LET YOUR BODY MOVE

One of the hardest things to explain to other people about bipolar depression is that it robs you of control—not just over your emotions, but over your body as well. There's a phenomenon called "psychomotor retardation" that occurs in many episodes: It can begin as a general slowing of your mental and physical processes and worsen into a near-paralysis. Of all the things I hate about depression, I think this tops the list.

I don't just mean that it's hard to move; I mean it's practically impossible. Let's say there's a bowl of frozen yogurt sitting in front of me, waiting to be eaten. I love frozen yogurt; I believe it makes the world a better place. But when I'm severely depressed, I can't summon up the energy or willpower necessary to grasp the spoon. The yogurt just sits in front of me, taunting me while it melts: "Who's frozen now?"

If I can't surmount the paralysis long enough to do something that gives me pleasure, imagine what it's like to face the unpleasant chores of daily living. Just the thought of getting out of bed plunges me into despair. Then there's the ungodly rigors of brushing my teeth. The torture of fluffing the pillows. The agony of buttoning my sweater. It's all beyond me, yet it has to be done and I swear to you, I've lain in bed for hours just trying to toss off the duvet so I can tackle life.

I've tried over and over to explain the horrors of psychomotor retardation to my doctors, friends, and anyone who will listen. I want them to see past my inert body and into my torpid brain. Maybe then they could truly understand that my failure to respond to messages, inability to socialize, lassitude, and lethargy are in no way voluntary. But no matter how much I plead for understanding, I always feel like I come up short. Like I'm whining about something ephemeral that's within my control—something I could master if I really tried.

I've really tried.

That's one of the reasons I get so upset when well-meaning people try to cheer me up by telling me about all the studies saying exercise can cure depression, or that it's at least as effective in treating it as antidepressants are. Invariably, these people forget an essential modifier that's used in all those studies: "moderate" depression. Believe me, if I were only moderately depressed I'd be the first one to jump up out of bed and go grab myself some sunshine. But when I'm depressed to the point of paralysis, I just hear that advice and blink with incredulity. They're kidding me, right? If I could move, would I be lying here helplessly enshrouded by my duvet? If I could move, why the hell wouldn't I?

Once when I was in the psychiatric hospital, I met a woman who was so depressed she was almost catatonic. She could barely blink, let alone groom herself or interact. Then her doctors tried a new drug on her, and I'll never forget what happened next. One morning before a therapy session, I watched her pull her comb from her purse and start to brush her hair. Long, fluid strokes in a smooth, even rhythm—so beautiful no ballet I've ever seen could possibly compete. With that movement, I knew that her depression had ceded control and she was in charge of her life again.

I often think of that moment when I'm bound by paralysis. I dream of the day when I, too, will simply get up and brush my hair.

THE BOTOX CURE

A study suggesting Botox may be a treatment for depression raised eyebrows, so to speak, at a recent American Psychiatric Association meeting. The study, conducted in Germany, showed a positive effect on the mood of patients who'd been injected with the toxin in certain facial muscles involved in emotion—particularly frown lines between the eyebrows.

As I understand it, the theory is that these muscles send feedback to the brain, reinforcing negative emotions by a frown or a furrow. But Botox prevents the muscles from moving, thereby stopping the signals from reaching the brain. The result: you look and actually feel less depressed. And significant results may be achieved with a single treatment.

Anthem Blue Cross, are you listening?

I didn't need a study to tell me that depression and appearance are closely aligned. After years spent in hospitals and mental health support groups, I can spot a depressed person from across the room. The sagging face always gives it away. I've often wondered: Does gravity affect depressed people more than others? Because that's what it looks like to me—like the weight of the world is pressing on the flesh, deepening the nasolabial folds and dragging the eyes and the mouth down, down, down.

I'm not immune to this phenomenon. I used to think I hid my depressions pretty well, behind a relatively composed and neutral countenance. But all the publicity I did for my books gave me a unique opportunity to see myself as others see me. In photo after photo, reel after reel, I saw what I looked like when I wasn't "on"— before the cameras started to click and my public face took over. It was a revelation that I'm still trying to process.

There was only one word for it: grim. And this was after a makeup artist got through with me, airbrushing out the wrinkles, simulating a healthy flush on my cheeks, making my eyes and skin glow. Sure, as soon as the red light blinked or the interviewer spoke to me, I instantly became animated and life and light poured back into my face. I flashed an eager smile. But until I knew I was being watched, I looked like my dog had just died.

What I wouldn't give to un-see those pictures, to forget that I ever looked like that. It shook me to my core because up until then I had truly believed that I passed for normal most of the time—that you'd never know, just to look at me, the sorrow that's burned through my soul. But there it was, for all the world to see and to judge.

It's taken me a while to develop some compassion for the sadness that's been etched into my face after so many years of struggling with depression. I suppose I could take the approach that these are my battle scars, honorably won and therefore something to be proud of. I suppose. For the time being, I'm just trying to remember to smile: not simply for publicity, but for the sake of my face. If there's such a thing as neuroplasticity for the brain, maybe my countenance can be retrained, too.

Botox may sound a bit Beverly Hills, and I doubt my insurance would go for it. But you know what? I think that study is right. Smiling doesn't just lift my eyes, it lifts my heart, as well. It's hard to feel truly miserable when my face refuses to participate in the gloom. Of course, sometimes it's simply impossible to smile, no matter how hard I try—it feels like a betrayal of my true emotions. But if stopping a frown can deceive depression, I'm all for cheating on myself. As Thích Nhất Hạnh put it, "Sometimes your joy is the source of your smile, but sometimes your smile can be the source of your joy."

— — —

HOORAY! I'M REALLY SICK!

For several months in a row a while back, I'd been flat-out exhausted. Not just tired—running on fumes. Worse yet, my mood was oscillating. After a long period of being relatively stable, I was ping-ponging between bouts of intense irritability and depression. Therapy once a week didn't help. Twice a week made me feel even crankier, mired in inertia and self-pity. It was time to call in the cavalry: my psychopharmacologist, the doctor who prescribes my medications and has the power to send me skyrocketing or plummeting, depending on the dose. I simultaneously admire and fear him.

With some trepidation, I left him a message, telling him I was cycling again. Just saying this to his answering machine made me feel like a bad patient, like I must have failed him somehow. A better patient would simply swallow her pills and be magically cured, to validate the magician. But he called me back immediately, and we pored over my list of meds, trying to find something to fiddle with.

My doctor's very cautious, and before he would adjust my dosage or try a new drug, he insisted I get some blood work done, to make sure I wasn't damaging my kidneys or doing other nefarious things to my body in my ongoing quest for sanity. I reluctantly complied, although needles scare me, the tests sounded expensive, and I was certain they would reveal one of those gruesome possibilities I'd read about online.

My doctor called me a few days later. "I got your labs back," he said.

Kidneys for sure, I thought, *or maybe my liver. Or cancer.* Google had said so. I sat down and gripped the arm of my chair. "What is it?"

"Your thyroid's completely out of whack," he said. "It's way below what it ought to be. That's probably what's causing your fatigue and low spirits."

Hypothyroidism! I wanted to kiss him. Only someone with a mental illness will understand my ecstatic reaction: This time it wasn't all in my head. What was happening to me was quantifiable—I could check it and chart it and predict its response. Whereas with bipolar disorder, you have to rely on assumption and faith because no one has discovered a definitive biomarker yet. If only there were a blood test, an X-ray, a saliva sample—something concrete a doctor could point to and say, "Yes, you're bipolar"—then no one could deny its existence. Until then, it's a cluster of symptoms dangling from a theory.

Treatment for my hypothyroidism was a breeze compared to the systematized torture I've come to expect from voodoo psychopharmacology, even at the hands of a brilliant physician. At one point, I was intimate with practically every antidepressant on the market because I'd slept with them all. Some of them twice. I know it's good that we have more options now, but it takes forever to comb through them—and when you're suicidally depressed, it's beyond cruel to have to wait six to eight weeks to know if a medication will give you relief. Then to start a new one, and wait again. And again, and again, until you hit the drug lottery. Or not.

There is at least reason to hope: I know that studies are in progress to determine whether a patient will respond to a particular drug, and how long it might take. Narrowing the field this way could revolutionize treatment, saving millions of dollars as well as millions of lives. But however well-intentioned, studies make promises that take too long to fulfill when patients are *in extremis*. It shouldn't have to be so hard.

For my thyroid, my doctor prescribed a single blue pill in the mornings. Tiny. One.

But without a doubt, the most amazing thing about my thyroid diagnosis was the total absence of stigma. I didn't have to lie about my symptoms or make up more socially acceptable ones, as I frequently feel forced to do with my bipolar disorder. I gleefully told everyone who'd been concerned about me, "I've got hypothyroidism!" and nobody blinked an eye.

I was blown away by my own hypocrisy. As a mental health advocate, I constantly espouse that depression is real, and that it's every bit as physical as diabetes, which also requires medication. I firmly believe this: I can feel the profound effects on my own body. And my belief is more than subjective. I've studied the research, talked with experts, even attended Grand Rounds lectures at teaching hospitals. Nothing has contradicted this truth: Depression is a real disease. And yet, I remained immensely relieved that I wasn't "just" depressed—that I had an objectively verifiable illness. *Shame on you*, I admonished myself.

But my heart was almost instantly lighter, and within a week I started feeling better. Not wildly so, but enough to realize how heavy the burden had been the past several months. And to understand that I still had a long way to go before I believed in my own wisdom.

— — —

SECTION III

User Precautions

STIGMA

"Mental illness is nothing to be ashamed
of, but stigma and bias shame us all."
—President William Jefferson
"Bill" Clinton (1946–)

"If you judge people, you have no time to love them."
—St. Teresa of Calcutta
("Mother Teresa") (1910–1997)

— — —

Over twenty years ago, the Surgeon General's report on mental health proclaimed that if we are ever to improve mental health and its treatment, we must address the problem of stigma, which so grievously "deprives people of their dignity and interferes with their full participation in society." This led to a diverse set of studies in the United States and around the world that sought to disentangle the phenomena underlying stigma.

One of the shared findings was that stigma is essentially a three-part process: stereotyping (i.e., negative labeling), prejudice (the emotional consequences of stereotyping, like fear and hatred), and discrimination (the behavioral reaction). This can occur on a personal, public, or institutional level, leading to disparate treatment—e.g., the allocation of fewer financial resources into the mental health system than into the somatic medical system. Perhaps this explains why the National Institutes of Health ranks research on the West Nile virus, which kills about 137 people a year, a higher funding priority than teen suicide prevention.

One of the most intriguing targets of the international studies was self-stigma—the practice of internalizing stereotypes and prejudice, generally to one's detriment. But as a University of Chicago study noted, a careful review of the research suggests a paradox: "Namely, personal reactions to the stigma of mental illness may result in significant loss in self-esteem for some, while others are energized by prejudice and express righteous anger." Those who became energized and outraged had "high group identification"—meaning they had come to accept their mental illness and to see the unjustness of others' negative responses.

This syncs with findings about the three main strategies that have been used to fight stigma: protest, education, and contact with the mentally ill. According to the European Psychiatric Association, "contact combined with education seems to be the most promising avenue" (https://www.ncbi.nlm.nih.gov/pubmed/16171984). In other words, when mentally ill individuals find the courage to disclose their illness to others, they combat both their own self-stigma and other people's harmful misconceptions. It's a powerful weapon against a life-threatening enemy.

DOC SHOCK

My long-term internist retired, and I went to see a new one because I had a burning pain in my upper abdomen, and I was afraid my ulcer had flared up again. I'm a very good patient, in my humble opinion. When I show up at the doctor's office I'm armed with my questions on a legal pad; I've done my homework. And I always present the doctor with his own typed copy of The List: an up-to-date compendium of all the drugs I'm on. I'm convinced that medicine should be an interactive process.

The List is a formidable creature, I'll be the first to admit. The medications I use for varying reasons take up almost a whole page. When I hand it over, I expect some degree of surprise: "You're taking all of these?" What I don't expect, and have no tolerance for, is judgment that predates the facts. Especially in a doctor.

Let's call him Dr. X. I wish you could see his office: swanky, with the latest in high-end modern art on the walls and all sorts of fancy diagnostic technology. He's maybe fifty and looks like he plays tennis or golf a couple times a week: nice tan, easygoing air. He took one look at The List and said, "What are you on all these for? You don't need to be on this, or this, or this. And you should get rid of this and this."

"I take those for my bipolar disorder," I said.

"But look at you." He scanned my chart. "You're a lawyer; you're a writer. You're a high-functioning person."

"I am now that I'm taking these meds."

He shook his head. "I don't believe it."

I spent the next fifteen minutes trying to convince him that (a) I was indeed bipolar; and (b) I needed to be on medication to treat it. A fairly significant amount of medication, I'll agree. But I defended each pill like the erstwhile litigator that I am because I believe in my treatment and my right to be sane.

I might as well have been talking to his stethoscope. He kept giving me backhanded compliments, saying I was "impressive" and "articulate." Hence I couldn't be mentally ill, was the none-too-subtle subtext. I finally lost my temper, something I'd never done with a doctor before.

"Look," I said, "I've written a whole book about my bipolar disorder, so I think I know it pretty well. Trust me, you don't want to see me off these meds. I've attempted suicide more times than I can count. I was hospitalized for three years. I've had electroshock therapy. I'm not fooling around."

I felt a hot flush suffuse my face as I fought back tears of frustration. The silence after I stopped speaking was so loud I could hear my pulse pounding in my ears. Dr. X put The List down and looked at me. "Well, if you're really bipolar, then I'd say this so-called ulcer must be anxiety, and it's just in your head."

He was lucky there were no sharp objects lying around. With a poise that belied my fury I stood up and thanked him for his time. I hate that I did that, but I was brought up to believe that doctors sit at the right hand of God. Certainly they've wielded enough power in my life that I respect their authority.

The minute I got to my car I called my therapist and told him what had happened. I asked for referrals to a new internist. Shaking, I ended the call. Then at last I started to cry. But these tears weren't as terrible as the ones I'd tried to suppress: They were as much of relief as anger. I wouldn't be seeing Dr. X again.

It disturbs me deeply whenever I encounter ignorance about mental illness. But this degree of cluelessness, from a man who has such tremendous influence over so many lives, shocked me. This was Beverly Hills, and I was a middle-class white woman; what on earth must the situation be like in less affluent places? Or for anyone who already faces discrimination based on race or sexual orientation? Socioeconomic status and language difficulties create enough barriers to treatment, without the further impediment of stigma from health care providers.

According to the Department of Health and Human Services' Office of Minority Health, ethnic minorities are critically under-represented in the provider population, which "often knows little about the cultural values and backgrounds of patients, or about the traditions of healing and the meaning of illness within different cultures." As a result of this lack of "cultural competence," the reported satisfaction with patient-physician interaction is significantly lower among people of color.

I thought about a badly depressed young black woman I'd met in the hospital, who came from South Central L.A. She'd told me that in her community, it was taboo to complain about mental health problems to anyone, even if you were fortunate enough to have access to care. "We survived slavery," she said. "What's a little sadness, compared to that? Just pray it away, I was told." And yet, the rate of suicide among young black men has risen 60 percent over fifteen years, and the suicide rate among young black women over the same period has risen a staggering 182 percent.

I also thought about all the LGBTQIA people I knew, struggling with such tenacity to come out of the closet, only to find that their battle against discrimination doesn't end there. A study of LGBTQIA mental health consumers found that they often felt compelled to hide their sexual orientation or gender identity in mainstream mental health settings, for fear that these issues would be used as further "evidence" that they were mentally ill. Hospital patients, especially in inpatient units and day programs, found that other patients were "frequently derogatory or even threatening" toward them, and that the staff was slow to discourage this behavior.

I witnessed this myself during my hospital stays. LGBTQIA patients often kept to themselves, not intermixing with the rest of the population. When I asked one young man why, he said he'd been warned by a male patient not to use the men's restroom; and that his own doctor had advised him "not to be too graphic" about his problems in group therapy sessions. Such homophobia and heterocentrism in the mental health system is particularly tragic, since the LGBTQIA community desperately needs intervention. LGBTQIA youth are more than twice as likely to feel suicidal, and over four times as likely to attempt suicide, as heterosexual youth, and 40 percent of transgender adults have attempted suicide in their lifetimes.

In this era of rapidly shifting demographics, it belies reason that only a privileged few should be able to obtain satisfactory mental health care. As a society, we rely on the sanity of all different types of people, now more than ever before. And we rely on our doctors to help us find and preserve that sanity. While many providers, if not most, are no doubt trying their best, it can sometimes be a dangerous trust. As James Baldwin said, ignorance allied with power is the most ferocious enemy there is.

THE RICH AND FAMOUS AND DESPERATELY SILENT

I had breakfast one morning with a Very Important Person, who happens to be bipolar. He's a gifted performer with a devoted fan base. I'd only met the VIP once before. I'd gone backstage after a performance, and for some reason, I can't recall why, I'd briefly referred to my bipolar disorder. He eagerly took me aside and whispered, "Me, too. We have to talk." And talk we did a few weeks later, nonstop and breathless for over two hours, our omelettes and coffee growing stone-cold.

We quickly learned we had loads in common. We laughed at the outrageousness of past manic adventures, and even held hands at one point in recognition of shared despair. I was surprised that our lives had followed such parallel tracks. There was the early abuse of alcohol in an attempt to self-regulate the highs and the lows. There was the flirtation with self-harm to release the otherwise unbearable pain. There was the guinea pig agony of medication trials, seeking just the right balance of chemicals to restore equilibrium. But there the striking resemblance stopped.

I was out and he was not, and the difference was fundamental.

"I'd never get work again," he said. Disclosing his mental illness would alienate his fans and the entertainment industry. In his opinion, bipolar disorder was a curse, with no point and no meaning. Why let the world in on his shame? Then he sat back in his chair, emphasizing the distance that had just opened up between us.

I tried to explain that we weren't as far apart as it seemed. For many years—for most of my life, I admitted—I'd felt the same way. I'd done whatever it took to hide my condition, until lying became as instinctive as breathing. He nodded; he knew what I meant. "So what finally made you change your mind?" he asked. His voice, that wonderful voice that has enthralled so many people, was calm. But I thought I detected a slight note of eagerness, too.

I had a moment's weakness: I wanted to tell him it was my hard-won courage, or my faith in humanity, or an overwhelming sense of decency, or some other noble reason that had inspired me to go public. I wanted him to admire me as much as I admired him. But I took a sip of cold coffee, and it was as bitter and bracing as the truth. I wasn't brave, I told him. I was desperate. I felt so trapped by my lies I couldn't remember anymore what was real and what was fabrication. The only way out was all the way out.

"Was it worth it?" he said. And then I heard it for sure: that faint tease of hope.

This part was sweet, and easy. I explained to him how much more rewarding my life has been since I've come out to the world: the avalanche of messages I've received thanking me for my example; the outpouring of genuine affection and concern; the astonishing stories that have come my way—so many of them, so inspiring. "People are desperate to hear that they're not alone," I said.

A flicker of light brightened his face for a moment, I'd swear to it. But then he shook his head, and I felt so sad. He was denying himself the gift of community, which was driving him further and further into secrecy and loneliness, and into his disease. Someday, he said, after his career was over, he'd really like to help others who were struggling. "Not now," he said. "But someday."

"You could have a tremendous impact on people," I told him.

Perhaps that appealed to his artist's narcissistic temperament. He smiled a crooked smile and looked at me. "I'm so tired of keeping it secret, worrying all the time that someone will find out," he said.

"I know," I said. "And all it takes are four little words: 'I have bipolar disorder.'" But we were done, and I knew it. I signaled for the check.

We hugged each other good-bye, and I wondered when or if I'd ever see him again. I hoped I hadn't gotten too close. Then again, I hoped I'd gotten close enough. I'd love to hear him sing something else, for all the world to hear.

SELF-STIGMA: WHEN
THE MIRROR LIES

Sometimes I think I'm making my bipolar disorder up. On a luscious morning like this one, when the white roses on my neighbor's trellis are flourishing and so am I, it's hard to believe I was ever the grief-stricken wretch I've written about so frequently. Happiness seems like the rabbit a magician suddenly whips out of his hat: It just appears, out of nowhere, and I clap my hands like a delighted child. I think, isn't life marvelous? Because I don't remember it ever being otherwise. Magical, yes. Miserable, no.

I can see why people go off their meds.

It may seem strange that I'd ever doubt my own mental illness, since I've published two memoirs about it and discussed it with people from all over the world. It's as much a part of my existence now as my freckles and red hair. I never question the fact that I'm a natural redhead. I never wake up in the morning and expect to be blond. So why then do I wonder if I'm bipolar? Why do I tell myself that it's a brand-new day and I feel just fine and whatever was I thinking?

This is not just my personal quirk—I've been plagued by other people's doubts, as well. Case in point: years ago, I was dating a psychologist. He was sexy and charming and easy to talk to—he had that wonderful soothing voice all therapists must learn in Therapy 101. So it wasn't surprising that things moved quickly between us, but I hadn't disclosed my condition to him yet. I wanted to wait until I was sure sex was in the offing. I thought it was important for him to know me then, just as I hoped he'd reveal himself to me.

One evening, after a prolonged bout of kissing, I knew the time had come. I pulled back and said, "If we're really going to do this, there's something I'd like to tell you."

"After," he whispered.

"No, I think we need to talk now."

"Good Lord," he said. "The need-to-talk line? So soon?"

I ran my fingers through his hair and smiled. "It's not that kind of talk. I just thought you should know that I've been diagnosed with bipolar disorder. It's pretty well controlled with therapy and medications, but I can be erratic at times."

Now he was the one to pull back. "You're not bipolar," he said. "I've seen plenty of people with bipolar disorder, and you don't fit the bill. You're a successful lawyer, for Christ's sake."

"But my doctor says—"

"Doctors misdiagnose all the time. We've spent a lot of time together, and while you may be intense and a little neurotic, I'm sure you're just as normal as the next person."

You'd be surprised at what the next person is hiding, I thought, but all I said was, "It hasn't been an easy road. But I'm much better now than I was before."

"You're better because you never were sick," he said.

I started to protest one more time, but he stopped me. "Less talking, more kissing," he said, and he took advantage of the sweet spot on my neck. *Well, nobody can say I didn't try*, I thought, and gave in to the momentum. We made love and it was fabulous and he never called me again.

Years later I ran into him at a dinner party. I was on the combative side of mania, so I asked him, "What the hell ever happened to us?"

"You were so convinced you were insane," he said. "And I knew you weren't. That felt creepy to me, like too much baggage."

I wanted to throw champagne in his face, but it was vintage and he wasn't worth it. But I wondered as I drove home, wiping off tears, *He's a doctor, and I'm not. Who am I to contradict him? Maybe he's right, and I'm just making things up.*

Self-doubt is poisonous—but when it spirals down into self-stigma, it can be deadly. Whole organizations are devoted to fighting stigma, but it's very hard to fight our own selves. I know, I've tried. When people question my bipolar disorder, they trample my reality. Even when I know they're wrong, it sets off a chain reaction of confusion in me. My self-confidence begins to crumble as I question my own veracity and my hard-earned belief in my illness.

I must be a liar, I tell myself. I must be pretending, to get attention. I'm a horrible person who doesn't know the truth from a lie anymore. The only thing I know for certain is that I'm somehow at fault for being me. If I truly wanted to be stable, I could because it's all just make-believe.

But it isn't. It's real, so real. That's what I always say when depression hits: "It's so real." I say this with a shake of my head and wonder in my voice because I simply can't believe how palpable the pain is. It's not only in my head, it's in my bones—my whole body aches with sorrow. I find this oddly comforting. It shows I'm not just a wimp who can't cope. I'm not a malingerer. It's not because I Googled "depression" one too many times. It's real.

And yet—on a day like today, when the happiness rabbit pops up unawares and I doubt that I was ever ill, I have to stop and email my therapist.

"Am I really bipolar?" I ask, for the umpteenth time in our relationship.

"Yes, you are," he writes back.

"Are you sure?"

"Yes, I am."

"Cross your heart?"

"I swear."

I'm convinced for the moment, but for that moment only. So I send myself a message for the future: "Note to self: it's real."

YOU MAY SOON BE UNREMARKABLE

A few years ago, when actress Catherine Zeta-Jones announced that she was bipolar, a frenzy of publicity erupted. That evening it was one of the lead stories on the *NBC Nightly News*, the nation's most popular news broadcast. I remember this because that morning a swarm of *Nightly News* cameramen had descended on my house. For several hours a reporter had earnestly interviewed me about "what it's really like to be bipolar."

I felt rather important and at the same time extremely weird, like I was a space alien asked to describe the customs and culture of my home planet. I did my best to explain the different mood states I travel through and the impact the illness has had on my life. I wasn't in top interview form that day—I was coming out of a depression and cursed the absence of my manic eloquence. But the reporter seemed very happy with the material he got. It wasn't until after the camera crew left that I realized why I was feeling so blue: because bipolar disorder was still considered big news.

I do want the illness to get as much attention as possible, from as many sources as possible. That's the way to more funding and research and hopefully, one day, a cure. And of course, it can be very valuable to witness other peoples' disclosures, so we don't feel alone. But I don't want bipolar disorder to be considered newsworthy because it's so bizarre. For every sober *Nightly News* interview, there's a flurry of tabloid exploitations, and God knows how many cyberspace atrocities. I look forward to the day when the condition will be so well known and understood that it borders on the mundane.

Another celebrity with bipolar disorder? Yawn. What else can we cover?

People from all across the country are eagerly waiting for that time to come. I constantly hear from bipolar readers how frightened they are that "someone will find out." They're certain they'll be fired or ostracized or no longer loved, so they hide an essential part of themselves from the world. These people live, not in a closet, but in a shoebox: stuffing their personalities into dark little fissures where enlightenment can never shine.

But then it happened: not too long ago, Zeta-Jones was in the news again. I barely caught the story. It was just a blip on the evening news—a photo of the actress, looking stunning as always, followed by a quick blurb: she was going to be hospitalized for "proactive treatment" of her bipolar disorder. Then the news moved on to the Middle East.

I wondered what proactive treatment was, and whether I could get it. Then it struck me—wham! pow!—how exceedingly short the whole story had been, if one could even call it a story. But why? Zeta-Jones was just as big a celebrity as she ever was. Yet this time around her bipolar disorder was treated more like a factoid, with a very pretty face attached. No reporters had called me for background material that day. Apparently no one wanted to go deep, as they say.

Because I used to work in the entertainment industry, I have some sense of when a story is hot, and when it's no longer a story. A few seconds on the nightly news constitutes interest, but the prurience of that interest is clearly waning. Maybe this means that being bipolar is not such a big deal anymore? Maybe people are getting used to it, and the stigma so many of us have had to endure all our lives is finally starting to lessen. I sincerely want to believe that. I want to be able to tell the people who write to me with such fear and distress: hold on, be patient, just wait. The end may be beginning, and you may soon be unremarkable.

TERMS AND DEFINITIONS

"Words are, of course, the most
powerful drug used by mankind."
—Rudyard Kipling (1865–1936)

"The misuse of language induces evil in the soul."
—Socrates (469–399 BC)

— — —

Mental illness is slippery and often defies comprehension. It's full of shadows and phantasms and inchoate feelings that need words to give them shape. Not just clinical terms, but everyday language that reflects everyday experience. And yet so much speech about mental illness is constrained. Sometimes it's the fault of political correctness (which has its place, except when it impedes clarity). Or the blurring intent of pharmaceutical agendas. Or, sadly, a lack of empathy and just plain fuzziness. Whatever the reason, imprecision and careless choices are dangerous to us all.

Celebrity suicides have highlighted that danger. After the extensive media coverage of Robin Williams's death in 2014, suicide rates spiked by 10 percent—a phenomenon called the Werther effect, which is essentially a technical term for copycat suicides and suicide contagion. This led experts to reconsider the rules of reporting, resulting in changes in the *Associated Press Stylebook*. It now cautions reporters not to explicitly describe methods, use graphic images or language, or otherwise sensationalize a death; and to provide resources to readers and, if possible, hope.

Some countries, such as Norway, don't report suicides at all in order to avoid any harmful consequences. But this seems to be taking prudence too far. Contrary to popular belief, a study by the Department of Psychological Medicine at King's College London found that simply talking about mental illness and suicide does not implant risky ideas in people's heads (https://www.ncbi.nlm.nih.gov/pubmed/24998511). Not talking about these subjects only intensifies stigma, impoverishes our language, and discourages people from seeking help.

Hard as it can be to open up about sensitive emotional issues, it's imperative that we do so. Men are four times more likely to kill themselves than women. It's impossible not to wonder how much of this tragic statistic is due to the stereotype that men are supposed to be strong—and silent.

CALL IT WHAT IT REALLY IS

One in five Americans is on some kind of psychiatric drug, mostly antidepressants. So all of you out there, dutifully taking your Paxil or your Zoloft or whatever, let me ask you: Do you know how hard it may be to go off it, should you ever want to? Did your doctor explain the risks when he dashed off that prescription, on the way to his next patient? Did you ever think to ask?

I didn't, which surprises me because as a lawyer, I'm naturally suspicious of all new developments. So every time my doctors prescribe a new drug, I whip out my legal pad and start taking notes. I ask what I can expect to feel, the possible side effects, interactions with food and other drugs, etc. I don't stop the interrogation until I feel satisfied. Then I go home and look it up online, which may or may not be such a good idea. But at least I tell myself I've done my homework before I pop that next pill.

I never think what might happen if I someday want to stop taking it. I'm too eager to be fixed, to be cosseted and soothed by the mighty magic that lives inside that tiny capsule—that symbol of hope and transformation. It's like starting out in a new relationship: you don't even think about the possibilities of divorce.

You should. Divorce is a messy business.

I'd been taking an expensive new antidepressant for about six months, with no discernible impact except on my checking account. My psychiatrist and I agreed we'd given the pill a fair shot, and its time was over. I started feeling sick three days after I reduced the dose. I'd only gone down a little bit because I knew that you should never, ever stop any drug abruptly. Ideally, you should slowly taper off in compliance with your doctor's directions, to give your body a chance to adjust to the change. Which is exactly what I did. Nonetheless, I felt woozy and nauseated, and when I tried to get out of bed, I fainted. Then the chills started, followed by a fever and copious sweating.

Definitely the flu, I thought, and I continued to go down on the drug. But every day I got sicker, until finally I couldn't keep anything down, not even water. Weeks passed, then a month, then two, and still I felt no better. But it never once occurred to me that going off the antidepressant might be the culprit. I didn't even think to call my psychiatrist because this was clearly physical illness, not mental: the province of my internist, gastroenterologist, and endocrinologist, although all of them were baffled.

Finally, when I found myself growing suicidally depressed, I called in my psychiatrist. He chided me for not calling him sooner. The medical term for what I was going through, he said, was "serotonin discontinuation syndrome." Serotonin is a brain chemical that may be implicated in depression, and antidepressants increase its availability. So when you go off an antidepressant, the amount of serotonin in your brain diminishes, and this can cause all sorts of nastiness. I read up on it: physical symptoms include problems with balance, gastrointestinal and flu-like symptoms, and insomnia. Psychological symptoms include anxiety, agitation, crying spells, irritability, and aggression. Some studies also reported "zapping" sensations in the brain, headaches, tremor, fatigue, and problems with vision, among numerous other things. In other words, pretty much anything that goes wrong with your mind and your body could be a result.

With the help of a magnifying glass, I scrutinized the teeny-tiny patient information pamphlet that came with my medication. Despite an alarmingly long list of side effects, there was no mention of "serotonin discontinuation syndrome" or of any of the problems inherent in reducing or stopping the dose. Getting angry at the drug company helped me a little. I was less angry with myself, at any rate, for not having asked the right questions of my doctor, and for my naive belief that prescription drugs aren't every bit as dangerous as street drugs.

But shifting the blame didn't lighten my symptoms. Nor did my doctor's admonition to be patient. Lying inert in a fetal position, unable to eat, sleep, write, or make any social commitments, I finally had to admit I was licked. My psychiatrist prescribed a different antidepressant to get me through the worst of the discontinuation syndrome, and gradually I started to feel more like myself.

I've had a lot of time to reflect on this experience, and I think in the end what upsets me the most is the misleading terminology being used to mask a significant, potentially life-threatening problem. While I was retching and shaking and passing out, I looked very much like one of those pathetic characters in a grainy 1950s film about heroin addicts kicking their habit. That squeaky clean clinical name "serotonin discontinuation syndrome" did nothing to capture the shame and degradation I felt for being so dependent on a drug. I really hate it when words don't work.

So it was some small comfort to discover in my research that "serotonin discontinuation syndrome" is a relatively recent term. Get this—it was coined at a pharmaceutical convention in 1996. Before that, what I went through had a very different name: It was simply called "withdrawal." The old words often work best, it seems, before they've been polished and prettified. "Withdrawal" would scare the hell out of any of us, and it's good to know when to be scared.

VAGUELY BIPOLAR

There are few things more frustrating than trying to describe the state of your mental health to someone else. It's amorphous and abstract; it defies pinning down. Clinical terms are practically useless—although, of course, you need to know them so that you and your doctor are on the same page. But they take a one-size-fits-all approach, which ignores the nuanced nature of my moods. I mean, come on: What *is* a "mixed state," anyway? Why can't I just say, I'm extremely agitated and mad as hell and I hate myself and you? Wouldn't a doctor get a clearer picture from that? Textbook speech is fixed and dry, and I'm a living, constantly evolving creature.

The right words at the right time can make all the difference, in unexpected and spectacular ways. Some of the best sex I ever had was with a young man I met in college, who was a dual English and premed major. He knew the precise names of all sorts of things I'd never dreamed existed. Up until him, the only sex-related word I knew was "no." But he gradually introduced me to the language of love, and his lessons made me delirious. Actually, at first they made me blush; then came the delirium. Since then, I've come to appreciate how essential it is to have *le bon mot* at hand.

But even though I'm a writer, the perfect description often eludes me, especially when it comes to my mental health. For example, right now I'm perched on the edge of a mood avalanche, for lack of a better term. I can sense that my world is about to change, but for the life of me I don't know in which direction. All I'm certain of is that the shift will be cataclysmic. And it's hard to explain this to anyone who's not bipolar, in a couple of curt or clinical phrases.

Like this morning—a good friend asked me how I was feeling. "Good," I said. "Fine." What I really wanted to say was something like, "You know that feeling when you walk into the ocean, and the sand begins to erode beneath your feet? It's exhilarating but scary because your balance gets tricky and you realize you're in the grasp of a force that's so, so much bigger than you. That's how I'm feeling, and that's what it's like to be bipolar, when your sanity starts to slip away."

But I didn't want to impose, and I didn't want her to think I was weird—I know most people don't live inside metaphors. Even here in Hollywood, the land of the well-spun story, people want to hear quick, to-the-point phrases they can easily understand. They want the elevator pitch, the beat sheet, the log line. It's a lazy way of listening—and besides, I don't have fast, easy summaries most of the time.

This isn't just wishful griping. A proper description is essential for the right diagnosis and treatment. How are we supposed to help our doctors care for us if we aren't given the time and permission to adequately express what's wrong? How can we recognize our symptoms and triggers if we can't explain them fully and clearly? The correct words aren't just empowering, they give you instant street cred, which is a nice thing to have when you're a mental health consumer.

So I vote for a vocabulary revolution! Let's ditch the one-word diagnoses and tell our doctors and loved ones how we're really feeling. This will undoubtedly require more than just a neatly packaged term or two from the DSM-5, which may make your pressed-to-the-minute doctor squirmy. But enough of the white coat worship. Sometimes you need a bit of a narrative, a glimpse of a story—"This is what happened to me today, and this is how it made me feel"—to make yourself understood.

I think the people who really care for us will be willing to listen because their level of frustration probably mirrors our own. They want to know how we experience our world, and I'm sure it's as hard for them to feel shut out by language as it is for us to feel so hemmed in. Let's allow ourselves to be heard and be truly seen. Let's claim all the orgasmic power that comes with knowing—and saying—just the right words.

SPITTING ON P.C.

I was invited to sit on a panel at the USC Film School. The topic was Mental Illness and the Cinema. My fellow panelists were film-makers; the moderator was a psychologist. I was the only person, I realized as I took my chair on the stage, who was mentally ill (or at least had admitted to it). I was the voice of madness. To do justice to the role, I tried not to look too composed—which wasn't hard because public speaking always makes me anxious.

The filmmakers had all made feature films or documentaries about some form of mental illness: depression, bipolar disorder, schizophrenia, etc. This being ultra-liberal Hollywood, the topic soon turned to political correctness. The moderator asked the film-makers if they'd had trouble with the diagnostic labels they'd placed on their characters. "That was one of the hardest things I had to deal with," one of them replied. "I didn't want to stereotype any-one." Another said, "I hated to use a diagnosis because it narrows the actor's range." Labels are bad, they all agreed. They harm people more than they help. The moderator concurred, saying that labels reduce the world to a cluster of symptoms defined by the DSM (the psychiatric bible).

The room glowed with that warm, we're-all-good-people-here vibe that sometimes comes over these events when everyone seems to be in accord. I was twitching in my seat, eager to speak yet keenly aware that I was a minority of one. But I couldn't help it, I've never been able to keep my mouth shut when I have a strong opinion.

"I'm really sorry to disagree with you all," I said. "But I think labels are great. I wouldn't be here if it weren't for my bipolar la-bel. I'd still be getting the wrong kind of treatment, and the wrong medications, and I'd probably have committed suicide by now. So if it's a choice between being labeled and being helped, I'll choose the label any time."

The audience fell dead quiet, as if someone had spit on their glow. Which I suppose I had. The moderator started to cut in, but I was just warming up: "And I don't care if that's the 'right thing' or not," I said. "We can't allow political correctness to get in the way of communication. Sometimes social change can simply be a conversation between two people. Let's just talk to each other, okay?"

Sweat was starting to form on my upper lip, and I could feel it snaking down my back as the room and the panelists and the moderator said nothing. And nothing still, for the longest moment ever. *Why do you always do this to yourself?* I thought. *Why choose advocacy as a career, when it makes you so uncomfortable?* But then, as if they'd been cued to react, the audience came alive and began to clap. Their applause felt deafening to me, and I wanted to do something dramatic, like drop the mic and leave the stage. But I didn't; I just blushed furiously.

Afterward, a swarm of people came up to me. I was expecting them to argue with my position, or at least to assert their own opinions about what's right and not right to say. But they didn't. Instead, to a person they thanked me: "I feel that way, too, only I don't like to say it," was the recurring theme of their comments. I could certainly empathize—I don't always like to say what I feel, either. But when silence can be construed as consent, I think it's a sin not to speak. Even, or especially, if it makes you sweat.

Instructions for Use

RELATIONSHIPS: GENERAL INSTRUCTIONS

"Everything that irritates us about others can
lead us to an understanding of ourselves."
—C. G. Jung (1875–1961)

"To know even one life has breathed easier because
you have lived. This is to have succeeded."
—Ralph Waldo Emerson (1803–1882)

Mental illness has an exponential impact. One in five adult Americans lives with a mental health disorder and comes into contact with scores more people, in varying degrees of intimacy. Loved ones are obviously most affected. A diagnosis is like a third party in any close relationship with a person who has a mental illness.

The American Psychological Association acknowledges that "it's normal [for loved ones] to feel a range of powerful—and often unpleasant—emotions," including shame, embarrassment, anger, self-blame, and guilt. Aberrant behaviors can be hard to understand and deal with, and it's tempting to believe that they are volitional, when in fact they are not. In a perfect world, this would be readily apparent; in the world as it is, we have to constantly work to remember that the illness is the enemy.

Difficult as any relationship can be, the marvelous thing is that friends and loved ones can make a profound difference in the life of a mentally ill person, by educating themselves and maintaining a positive attitude. They can contribute mightily to recovery—not only improving that person's life, but maybe even saving it. The investment is significant, but the dividends are so rewarding.

DON'T FIX ME, I'M NOT BROKEN

The number one symptom of depression for me is my inability to get in the shower. Once I'm in there I'm okay, but it takes a gargantuan effort on my part just to turn on the faucet. I lie in bed contemplating that simple movement of twisting the knob; nothing, and I mean nothing, can incentivize me to actually do it. I know I'm not alone in this because I've Googled "hating the shower" and there's a whole community out there that identifies with this phenomenon.

I was struggling with it again when a good friend called me. He knows about my bipolar depression and is pretty well educated about its symptoms and triggers. I told him I was having trouble getting up and getting into the shower, and to his credit he asked, "Why?" I stumbled into an explanation of how much I despise the sensation of the water striking my bare skin. That my nerves are too sensitive to take that onslaught. That it feels like an invasion, a flogging, or at least some kind of corporal punishment.

"You need to get a new shower head," he said. "One that feels like a gentle rainfall. Just go on Amazon and look around. They have hundreds of options, you'll find something there."

The last thing I needed was hundreds of options. Nor could I imagine myself expending the energy necessary to scroll down endless screens when I could barely move.

"Yes, but I'm too depressed to use the computer," I said.

"You're being your own worst enemy," he said. "Just go look for the right shower head, and they'll deliver it straight to your door. You don't have to do anything but help yourself."

I didn't want to help myself. I wanted to lie in bed and moan about how I couldn't get in the shower. I did my best to explain this.

"It's not about the stupid shower head or the way the water comes out," I said. "It's me; I can't go through the ordeal."

"You could if you had the right kind of spray," he said, beginning to sound annoyed.

"No, I couldn't."

"You won't even try." I could hear the disgust and anger mounting in his voice, which frightened me. He's an integral part of my support system, and I couldn't risk his abandoning me, which has happened before when he's gotten mad. I realize deep down that it's his frustration at not being able to cure my depression that really bothers him, but that knowledge came later and didn't help me in the moment.

"I *would* try, but I'm too depressed," I said. I also realize how irritating depressed people can sometimes be, with their inevitable "Yes, but" responses. Yes, but . . . Okay, but . . . I can hear when I'm doing it, but that never seems to stop me.

"Now you're just being stubborn," he said.

"Maybe, but you don't understand. It's the forward movement that's required; I can't bring myself to face it."

"You could if you had the proper shower head," he insisted, and I sighed and gave up.

"Fine, I'll go look on Amazon and see what they have," I said, knowing that I'd never get within fifty feet of my computer that day.

"I have to go now," he said, and hung up without saying good-bye.

I was so frustrated I started to cry. This was one of the few people in my life who understood my illness, who'd read everything I've written on the subject, and knew my essential rule for when I'm depressed. I've repeated it over and over, but I guess it needs to be said again because it's so contrary to human—especially male—nature.

The rule is just this: Don't try to make it all better. Don't cheer me up or attempt to talk me out of it. Just let me talk about my pain. I don't know why this works so well, I only know that it does. It's so simple: I don't want to be fixed—I'm not really broken. All I want is to be heard.

Yes, but . . . It can be so hard to listen.

RELATIONSHIPS ARE SIMPLE: NEVER DO THIS

Hello out there, normies! That's insider's lingo: what many members of the bipolar community affectionately call those of you who don't have a mental illness (or haven't been diagnosed with one yet). You're reasonably sane, relatively predictable. You're the control group in those double-blind studies. You've got it all going on, except . . . Sometimes you run across those of us who aren't considered—quote, "normal"—and you just can't figure us out. Maybe we're your best friend, your employee, your boss, your sibling, your child, your lover. You'd really like to treat us well, but let's face it: We can be hard to understand. We're ticklish emotionally. We do strange things and don't even realize it. It's not always easy dealing with us. We know. So here are some insider's tips—a few things you should avoid doing at all costs in a relationship with a bipolar person:

1. NEVER THROW PLATITUDES AT US

When I first started practicing law, I noticed that a great many lawyers relied on boilerplate language: phrases or even whole documents that had been used before, so many times they weren't even looked at anymore, just skimmed over in a brief. One day I asked a senior partner why the use of boilerplate was so endemic, and he told me, "Real writing means you have to actually think. Who has time for that?"

Take the time. Think. Don't subject a bipolar person to the dregs of your intellect. If he's going through an episode, don't tell him, "It's all in your head," or "Everything will look better in the morning," or "Time heals all wounds," or "Try making lemonade out of lemons" (a good friend actually said that), or the zillion other platitudes that are unfortunately available.

With kindness, look the situation in the face and let your words reflect what you see. Bipolar people have been subjected to so many clichés in place of concern, they'll appreciate any effort on your part to express what you're really feeling.

2. NEVER THINK THE ILLNESS DEFINES US

I think whether someone elects to say "I am bipolar" vs. "I have bipolar disorder" is strictly a personal choice. But it's inescapable that once you've been diagnosed, the condition becomes part of your life. Some people are more symptomatic than others, of course, so for them it plays a bigger role. For me, it's a constant companion. That said, I am so much more than my diagnosis, and so are all the other bipolar people I know. I accept the illness as a part of my identity—it's the lens through which I see the world, and for a writer that's essential—but a slice is not the whole. Being bipolar doesn't exclusively define me any more than, say, my passion for Sherlock Holmes does.

That's why stereotyping a bipolar person is sure to lead to misunderstanding and mistakes. If I've learned anything from the slew of people I've met, there is incredible variety in the bipolar universe. We are not just "the mentally ill." We are doctors and lawyers and students and teachers and politicians and celebrities and entrepreneurs and artists and I could go on forever. The illness plays no favorites. But if you must stereotype us, consider this: people with bipolar disorder skew highly intelligent and unusually creative—and are always intriguing, if you're bored with the obvious.

3. NEVER UNDERESTIMATE THE DANGER

Numbers tell it like it is. Here's what studies have shown:

- At least 25 percent to 50 percent of bipolar individuals will attempt suicide at least once;
- Over their lifetimes, the vast majority (80 percent) will have suicidal ideation; and

- 75 percent of people who died by suicide expressed suicidal feelings in the weeks prior to their deaths.

In my own life, I've earnestly attempted to kill myself several times. Sometimes the pain is just so bad, death seems like the kinder option. I'm much better now, but I share these facts because you need to know that suicide is a real and ever-present risk with bipolar disorder. People don't just talk about it; they do it. An attempt isn't merely a cry for help—it should be considered a clarion call to action.

So if someone you know or love talks about suicide, even jokingly or in a passing remark, don't get angry. Stop and listen. Ask him if he has a plan. Ask if he's stockpiled medication or has a gun in the house. Ask how you can help—even, or maybe especially, with menial tasks, like doing laundry or picking up a prescription. Sometimes the smallest alleviation of daily stress can work wonders where suicide's concerned. Above all, take it seriously. The statistics do.

4. NEVER GIVE UP HOPE

When I'm far, far gone down the blackest hole of depression, I know the phone will eventually ring, forcing me to move. Or when I'm so high my ceiling can't contain me, I know I'll eventually have to come down to answer the persistent chimes of a text. I have people in my life who love me, and they annoy me when I most want to be left alone. God bless them. They refuse to go away.

To be frank, I don't get it. I probably would have given up on me around about the third suicide attempt. But no, they hang on. They drive me to the doctor, they read about the illness, and they listen with their hearts wide open. They tell me stories that start out, "Once you're feeling better . . ." and they look me in the eye while they're saying that. They believe in me, and in a future that doesn't revolve around doctors and drugs and hospitals.

And I believe them because they're supposed to be "normal" and so they must know what they're talking about. That's why if you want to be in a rewarding relationship with a bipolar person, you must never, ever give up hope. You must hold it in trust for those of us whose vision is slightly blurred, who can't quite see the path, who need a dose of hope every now and then to make it through the day.

ETIQUETTE FOR THE ORDINARY

My mother once told me, "If you were the witness to a lineup, you'd always pick the guilty man." She wasn't praising my perspicacity; she meant I go for men who've been in trouble. True enough. The men I like usually do have some history, enough scars to tell good battle stories—provided those scars are in the process of healing. I admire anyone who's in recovery, of any form. To be in recovery means you have to admit that you've got a frailty, and I think that bodes well for any relationship. I'm drawn to people who have the courage to surrender.

But many of the people in my life aren't in recovery and don't have any official mental health diagnosis. Ironically, I often find these "ordinary" relationships to be far more difficult than the ones with the so-called difficult people. I have to explain things that seem perfectly obvious to me, simple things like feelings are there to be probed, not ignored; introspection isn't narcissism, it's necessary. They disagree with me, sometimes vehemently, because they haven't known what it's like to be hijacked by emotion and the disaster that can result.

It isn't their fault that they're ordinary. It isn't my fault that I'm not. But the clash between the two extremes gives me a walloping headache sometimes. There must be better ways for us to get along, and I think the answer may lie in good old-fashioned etiquette. It is, after all, the great social lubricant.

Ever since I was a little girl, I've collected books on etiquette in an attempt to demystify the polite norms that everyone else seemed to take for granted—yellowing, dog-eared editions about how to properly nibble a canapé, how to hide your handkerchief up your sleeve, or gracefully dispose of an offending piece of gristle. Such information comforted me no end, and I used to peruse those books for hours, happy in the knowledge that in this tumultuous, chaotic world I at least had mastery over a moment of gristle.

But manners are about so much more than knowing how many tines there are in a salad fork. Good manners help us converse with other people. They suggest how to physically interact. They smooth the rough edges of close contact. So, in the spirit of rapprochement, let me tell you how I would like to be treated by ordinary people when difficult situations arise.

It's tempting, when I'm upset, to throw my diagnosis at me. For example, an ex-boyfriend of mine used to rile me up all the time. He was devious, insensitive, and a host of other things that his gorgeous green eyes eventually didn't make up for. I'd behave like most people when I got angry at his misbehavior: fast words, furious emotion, tears. It was catnip to him. "You're wrong!" I'd sputter. "You're cycling," he'd say.

For good reason, most bipolar people are skittish about revealing their illness—including me, and I've been ridiculously public about my travails. The problem is, we never know when stigma will erupt, so we live in silence way too much of the time. Even I don't discuss the daily details of my condition with just anyone in my personal life. I choose, quite carefully, who gets to know what, and I'm thrilled when they want to know more.

But when someone I've confided in tries to use that information as a weapon against me—watch out, we're in for big trouble. Knowing about my illness is a sacred trust. Please don't abuse it. Because hey, sometimes I'm not manic at all. Sometimes I'm just dead right.

Another situation that always causes difficulty is when people repeatedly insist that I try this or that remedy because "It's natural. It can't hurt you—they sell it at Whole Foods." How many times have I heard that one? I suspect most bipolar people have. And how many times have we gone out and bought that vitamin, that supplement, that herb, etc., only to find out that it triggers mania, or adversely interacts with our other medications, or is in some way deleterious to our mental health?

It's axiomatic: Just like prescribed drugs, these substances can affect the brain's chemistry (that's why you buy them, after all) and therefore may also have bad side effects. In fact, according to the *New York Times*, there are numerous cases of serious and even lethal side effects from herbal products. Worse yet, manufacturers of nonprescribed substances don't need FDA approval to market their products. There's no quality control, and no pressure on them to 'fess up the truth.

I know that people who recommend these things mean well, but "natural" doesn't always mean safe. So please resist the urge to play doctor—it's dangerous, and bipolar people are sometimes too desperate to grasp that.

Well-meaning people are also quite voluble on my need to exercise when I'm very depressed. I know, I know. I know all about that clinical study that showed exercise can be just as effective for moderate depression as antidepressants. I think it's wonderful. I'd be out there in a minute pumping iron and doing push-ups and swimming laps and working myself up into a therapeutic lather, if only I could move. There's the rub: My brain sincerely wants my body to move, but my body refuses to listen. If I could manage to do a Warrior One, I wouldn't be depressed. So let me rest. Breathing in and breathing out is challenging enough.

Now here's a more delicate situation. When I get really happy about something—it happens, I'm human—people who aren't bipolar often try to kill my buzz. Doctors and friends look at me with worried faces and warn me that my mood is changing, that I may be too chipper for my own good. It makes me want to smother my joy, and leaves me feeling alone, embarrassed, and misunderstood.

I get it, to a certain extent. Sometimes it's hard for even me to distinguish between safe euphoria and the beginnings of a dangerous manic episode. Only time can truly tell for sure (although one good clue is, has something objectively wonderful happened? If so, we can probably all rest easy). But that doesn't mean I don't just wake up out of the blue some days and feel all bright and sparkly for no reason, and want to share my elation with the world. I shouldn't be deprived of my fair portion of dizzy-headed delight. For that brief period of time when I'm in a plain old good mood, please, let me enjoy it. I've probably earned a tryst with happiness.

At its core, etiquette is based on consideration for the other person's feelings. Or as my 1938 first edition of *Manners for Moderns* says, "Politeness is to do and say/The kindest thing in the kindest way." If I were to step out tomorrow into a society where everyone had pledged to honor that maxim, I'd be eager—no, hell, I'd be thrilled—to make its acquaintance.

RELATIONSHIPS ARE SIMPLE: JUST DO THIS

I'm frequently asked, "What's the best way to love someone with bipolar disorder?" Usually the person asking me has the traces of a frown on his face. I empathize. We're not the simplest bunch of souls, the 5.7 million of us with bipolar disorder. But then, simplicity isn't what you fell in love with in the first place, is it?

No. Most likely you were attracted to the volatility, the edginess, the uncertainty. Loving someone who's bipolar means loving a panoply of characters: the girl who's overcast one morning and the one who's radiant by mid-afternoon. There's an excitement about never being able to predict the emotional weather; it calls on all your relationship skills.

So what does it take to love a bipolar person? A little specialized care and feeding. We may be challenging at times, but if you're after easy, superficial emotions, perhaps you should look elsewhere. Or, at least, read on.

1. LET A DEPRESSED PERSON BE DEPRESSED

Depression is a powerful demon, one that demands its rightful due. It may skulk away in its own good time, but while it's present you have to acknowledge it. Telling a depressed person they're not depressed, or that they have no reason to be, is simply illogical and rude. Ask the person how they feel, and then listen—really listen—no matter how hard it may be not to interrupt. This is where trust, that frailest of flowers, begins to take root.

2. EDUCATE YOURSELF ABOUT THE ILLNESS

If you were dating someone from Spain, you'd learn a few words of Spanish, right? The same reasoning applies. Bipolar disorder is a strange and exotic world, and it's very lonely and frightening to feel like you're traveling through it solo. I guarantee you that the respect and love you exhibit by learning the basics of this condition—elementary things, like the difference between mania and hypomania—will pay off in spades. All the people I've ever adored have asked me about my illness with genuine curiosity. They know what rapid cycling looks like, and which events are likely to be triggers. Sometimes they can even help me identify what mood I'm in when I'm not quite sure myself.

3. APPRECIATE THE UNEXPECTED ADVANTAGES THAT BIPOLAR DISORDER BESTOWS

Far too many bipolar people live secret-shrouded lives, and never get to exhibit the amazing gifts they've been granted along with the intense mood lability. If you can establish the rapport necessary for the bipolar person to open up and show you what's really going on inside, I think you'll be surprised. It's a dangerous disease but it has its perks, like a bad job with good benefits. Creativity runs rampant through bipolar blood. Bipolar eyes see the world in a unique and fascinating way. And because we've known what it's like to struggle, we're very generous with our empathy. If you love someone with this illness, you're only a heartbeat away from sharing these riches.

4. REMEMBER THERE'S A TOMORROW

It's scary when symptoms manifest, and it's frustrating for everyone when they don't go away. But the weird blessing of bipolar disorder is that it's in constant fluctuation. Eventually, a mood will shift, or a medication will start to take effect. I know this intellectually; I forget it instantly when I'm suffering. What I need the most when I'm going through an episode is to hear from someone I trust that relief is coming down the line. In the midst of my pain, I'm not always capable of sustaining that belief, so someone else has to be its custodian. A simple reassuring reminder that change is inevitable—it's happened before, and will happen again—works wonders for my recovery.

Loving someone with a bipolar diagnosis may be one of the most intriguing things you ever do in your life. It's a quest well worth the treasure because bipolar feelings run deep and true. I grant you: the course isn't always smooth. But when is it ever, with love?

— — —

RELATIONSHIPS: SPECIFIC INSTRUCTIONS

"You don't develop courage by being happy in your relationships every day. You develop it by surviving difficult times and challenging adversity."

—Epicurus (341–270 BC)

"Love is no assignment for cowards."

—Ovid (43 BC–AD 17)

How do you deal with someone who's floridly manic, or desperately depressed, or severely anxious, or suicidal? Or worse yet, in denial of any or all of the above problems? These are real conundrums that demand real-world, practical solutions. But for most of us, that means giving advice, and therein lies a conundrum all its own.

Rather than helping people in trouble, advice can often backfire. It can constitute what author Robert Bolton defines as "a roadblock in interpersonal communication." It can even activate the brain's limbic (threat) system, by signaling challenges to our status and autonomy. Research on reactance theory shows that whenever someone tells us what to do and how to do it, we respond with defensive defiance (https://www .psychologytoday.com/us/blog/do-the-right-thing/201407 /giving-people-advice-rarely-works-does).

That's why "You should" is a terrible way to start any sentence. It inevitably places the advice-giver in a superior position. "I know better than you," it says. Not that people consciously intend to create these dominant/submissive roles. But it's a sad if undeniable truth that you can mean extremely well and hurt someone anyway.

So—and the irony is thick here—don't give advice is sometimes the best advice, even in the most challenging relationships. But there are other ways of helping that don't elicit the same knee-jerk defiant reaction. Instead, listen closely. Educate yourself thoroughly about the situation, so you can explore possible options. Ask thoughtful questions. Consult experts. Encourage the person's own sound contributions. Model the behavior you hope to inspire. (See the *Harvard Business Review* for more tips on this "subtle and intricate art," at https://hbr.org/2015/01/the -art-of-giving-and-receiving-advice.) You'll learn far more about the person and the problem than you ever would have if you had simply resorted to giving advice.

LIMITING MANIC FALLOUT

Here's what it's like to be around me when I'm manic, according to witnesses who have seen it and survived. It's like talking to Minnie Mouse: The timbre of my voice goes way up and my speech is pressured, as if something were goading me to chatter at hyperdrive speed. You find the machine gun rapidity of my ideas and emotions delightful at first, even inspiring. You can almost see what I insist upon: that there are connections everywhere, to everything. We hold chaos theory conversation—from Manet to butterflies to trade policy with Mexico, all in the flicker of a few sentences.

You're flattered by the intensity of my attention—the way I touch you frequently to make my point, and sear you with my eyes, which are only for you. You feel incredibly witty and fascinating because I seem thrilled by everything you contribute, eagerly interrupting to question you further. And all the while you're talking to me I'm in motion, pacing or tapping my fingers or jiggling my legs. Energy radiates out of me and galvanizes everyone in my vicinity. You can't help but think, *I'll have what she's having.*

But at some point our conversation evolves into pure self-expression because my ideas become too scattershot to follow. That's when things begin to shift. Where you once felt engaged in an intense rapport, you now feel left behind. This gives way to an unsettling sense that something is off, something doesn't quite feel right. You realize you're no longer a participant in a dialogue, but strictly an audience for my grandiose proclamations and visions. You exist only as a vacuum to suck my words up.

If you're a stranger, you may decide at this point to exit the interaction altogether, and feel relieved if guilty about your escape. Don't worry, I probably won't even remember our encounter. But if you're a loved one and are committed to seeing this through, then you should be aware that you've now crossed into dangerous territory. As with any risky expedition, it's important to know the obstacles ahead and steer clear of them whenever possible.

Let me draw you a map, so you can avoid the worst patches of quicksand.

In mania, people are drawn to speed and excitement and anything rash. So keep me away from riptides and the edges of cliffs, both actual and metaphorical. Do your best to stop me from drinking or driving or dating (there are no sexual limits in mania). Shopping—especially online shopping because it's instant gratification—is particularly fraught and should be actively discouraged. This can be hard because money feels like an infinite resource to me then, however strained my finances may actually be. I shower it on everyone: valets and waiters get jaw-dropping tips. I may give my entire wallet to a homeless person on the street, but not without first eliciting his life story and communing with his universe.

Maybe you'll get lucky and be able to redirect my raging seductiveness toward you, assuming you're my lover already. But don't make the mistake of submitting to my advances if we've only ever been friends. You'll probably enjoy it, but regret it later. Try to shift my focus to something that uses up my excess energy but doesn't get me into trouble—like writing the Great American Novel, or cleaning my house (or better yet, cleaning yours). Any kind of organizing is great: filing in particular attracts manic people like flies; it's a real buzz. Music, of the right kind, can also calm turbulent passions. Avoid the Sex Pistols, bring on the Bach.

Mostly, I shouldn't be left to my own devices—and that's where all the trouble starts. You have to explain to me why I can't just follow my impulses, and that means using the loaded phrase, "Because I think you're manic." Telling a bipolar person she's manic is like telling a falling-down drunkard he's had enough. True, perhaps, but them's fightin' words. I'll resent you and hate you and not hesitate to tell you so, loudly and in public. I'm a real challenge to be around then, although I'll eagerly debate you on that: I'm right, you're wrong, and my trump card is, you don't know what it's like to be bipolar so shut up.

So why are you still hanging around? Is it worth all this energy and aggravation to save one soul from herself? This is where you have to know your own limits, and be the conscience and the memory of the relationship. You have to understand that none of this outré behavior is volitional, even if it looks like free will run riot. It's the symptom of an illness, a nightmare that must and will come to an end . . . But where? In a foreign country, or in some stranger's bed? By intervening, you protect a sick person's safety and dignity. It's a noble act, however little it may be appreciated at the moment.

Ultimately, the best counsel I can give you for dealing with someone who's flagrantly manic is to put up storm walls when symptoms aren't present. Make a solemn contract with your loved one that if things get too out of hand, it's okay for you to call their doctor— and make the doctor aware of this in advance. Get the person to write down ahead of time: "I give you permission to tell me I'm manic." With this blind trust comes an inherent promise that you won't use their illness against them, ever. You promise to fight fair.

In truth, it's very hard for me to know with absolute certainty what it's like for you when I get manic because I'm too flooded by my own sensations to take anyone else's into account. The foregoing is based on hearsay, and while I trust my witnesses, I can only see the situation from my point of view. I accept that it's a difficult undertaking. I accept that it's a severe test of tolerance. But after a lifetime of relying on the courage of others to protect me, I have to admit: I don't believe in tough love. I simply believe in love. It's the only reason I'm still here.

TELL ME WHERE IT HURTS

When you're depressed, it often feels like nothing anyone can say will make any appreciable difference. And sometimes that's true. When you're really, really down, you simply can't take it in: your ears are too full of other sounds, harsh grating noises only you can hear. But one thing truly does make a difference. I've written about this time and time again, but I'm going to keep repeating it until I think it's finally caught on.

Have your loved ones say these five little words: "Tell me where it hurts."

I've begged everyone around me to please, please remember that simple phrase. Don't tell me I'm imagining things. Don't remind me that a few weeks ago I was all moonbeams and lilies. Don't recommend your homeopathic remedies, your cat videos, your diet, your faith. Don't tell me about your sister's best friend's boyfriend's niece, who was cured by Pilates. Please, if you love me, just say, "Tell me where it hurts." Then sit down and really listen.

Granted, it's not an easy option, but it's essential if you want to help. There's something surprisingly healing about spewing forth the poison that's been brewing inside, the acid corroding the soul. When darkness hits the light it can't help but evaporate a little bit, and sometimes that little bit can mean the difference between giving up and going on.

I know this runs contrary to every impulse. It's human nature to flat-out refuse to hear that life is no longer worth living. It's human nature to contradict someone when they tell you there are no options left. But do your best to suppress that urge because you'll only stoke the fire. Depression thrives on proving everyone's wrong, that the world is a genuine cesspool. And believe me, depression's a wily beast, because it isn't bound by reason. It's capable of convincing the Pope himself that life is nasty, brutish, and short.

"I love you and I want you to live" is a fine response to whatever you hear, no matter how many times you have to say it. Love isn't constrained by logic, either, and sometimes it's able to sneak past vitriol and seep straight into the heart. Maybe not right away, but in the nick of time. "I love you and I want you to live" is one of those phrases I've found myself remembering in the dead of night when I'm about to start counting out too many pills. It makes me pause for just that moment it takes to breathe another breath, then maybe another, until I find the infusion of air I need.

A word of caution: The veneer that separates depressed and so-called normal minds isn't that thick. If you ask a severely depressed person where it hurts, you're almost certain to hear things that will frighten you, truths about life that in polite company almost always remain unspoken: like how helpless we all are against the unknown, and the inevitability and imminence of decay. Some say this harsh realism is what made depressives like Abraham Lincoln and Winston Churchill such great wartime leaders. Their vision encompassed not just glory, but gore.

So proceed with care, but don't let it stifle your compassion. Remember why you're asking where it hurts: because you want to lessen your loved one's pain. That goal is so exalted it will strengthen and protect you. Love may not always be wise, but it's one hell of a weapon—and never forget, this is war.

— — —

IS DEPRESSION THE
NEW PLAGUE?

When a bad depression looms, it's like seeing that tornado in *The Wizard of Oz* coming straight at me. My very first instinct is to jump into my imaginary basement and hide for dear life. It's soothingly dark in the basement; best of all, I'm alone. No one can ask anything of me—I can't hear the phone or the knock on the door or the computer's nagging alerts. It's just me and the fear and the frenzy, at least until it passes and it's safe for me to emerge again.

For years, people have complained about these extended absences I take from life. But my avoidance still seems worth it to me—more than that, it seems inescapable. When I'm depressed, I can't engage in meaningful conversation. In truth, I can hardly speak. If you've never been seriously depressed, I doubt you'll understand this. If you have, you're probably nodding. At my most depressed, I'm Garbo-esque: I desperately want to be alone. But I also want—I need—to know that I'm loved, that somebody out there cares about me no matter how convinced I am that I'm the dregs of the earth and warped at my core and don't deserve to breathe. It's taken me years of therapy and countless mistakes to make this blatant contradiction work. Here's a quick summary of what I've learned:

First of all, it's up to me to send a short message to the people who might be concerned about me, saying, "I'm going through a depression. I'll be back in touch when it passes." That may sound easy, but it takes enormous willpower to write those two trifling sentences—because it means that I've finally admitted to myself that I've crossed over to the dark side, that it's back again and I'm about to be imprisoned in Oz. This is a terrifying realization, hence

I usually never get around to writing that all-important communication until things are at their bleakest.

When I do manage to send it though, the responsibility shifts—and somehow this is the point where it all gets screwed up. For the first few days, I get inundated by calls and texts and emails that I can't return, containing insistent, intrusive offers to visit, bring me movies, take me out to dinner. I know people sincerely want to help, but if I could go out to dinner, for Christ's sake, I wouldn't have had to send that message in the first place. I also get tons of well-meaning advice, and there's nothing more demeaning and distancing than hearing "you should" when you can't.

Or else, most mystifying of all, I get silence, the very last thing I want to hear. Nothing. Not a word, not an inquiry, not a whisper of hope—from people who supposedly adore me. It breaks my frayed and aching heart, and is a complete enigma to me. How can anyone know that a loved one is going through hell and not reach out to comfort them? I don't get it; I never will. I've talked to my therapist about this, and he told me, "People are afraid of complicated emotions. They're afraid they'll be caught up in the depression." I think the more likely explanation is what I always hear when I come back to life: "I thought you wanted your space." Yes, but not a vast, empty void.

I realize that helping someone who's depressed is a very complex scenario, but there are some simple answers. If you who worry that you may not be doing enough, let me tell you what has really worked for me:

1. Leave a quick check-in message on my voicemail: "I love you. This will pass." Or,
2. Send me a short email or text: "I love you. This will pass."
3. Repeat as necessary.

Anything along those lines would mean the world to me. You're not asking me to do what I can't. You're not arguing with me about how I feel. You're just reminding me that I'm alive, and that it matters to you. Even if it doesn't to me.

— — —

IT ISN'T "JUST" ANXIETY

Very often a mental illness diagnosis doesn't travel alone. It's accompanied by other diagnoses: anxiety, in my case, or substance abuse, or eating disorders, etc. This is such a common occurrence there's a special word for it: "co-morbidity." A scary-sounding word and a troubling situation, which makes everything more difficult: diagnosis, treatment, recovery, and especially relationships. It's hard enough to learn how to deal with one disorder, without the extra curve.

Last week I'd made plans to go to lunch with a friend, but that was before I was besieged by intense anxiety. What was I feeling so anxious about? Everything, nothing, I didn't know. Vague, restless spirits were blackening the sky, and calamity was coming, that was all I was sure of. I called my friend and told him how I felt so he could back out of the lunch if he wanted to—because my anxiety, if not handled properly, can devour everything in its presence. He took me up on my offer. He's seen me anxious before.

I was hurt, but I wasn't surprised. Despite its harrowing nature, anxiety seems to be the least respected of the mental illnesses. Depression is now recognized as having a physical component. Schizophrenia and bipolar disorder have achieved a certain gravitas. But anxiety? Please. Get over it.

Everybody gets anxious, or so they think. And they deal with it. So why the fuss? Obviously, we need a different word to describe the nightmare that is clinical anxiety. It bears little resemblance to the garden-variety jitters everyone is familiar with. When I'm anxious, it's almost worse than being depressed. It's like a metronome is lodged in my brain, ticking off potential disasters. That endless litany of "what if, what if" crowds out any thoughts that might be useful or soothing.

Most people get anxious about specific things, and when those things get better, the disquiet disappears. But with generalized anxiety disorder—which affects at least 6.8 million adults in the United States—there's no apparent cause for the apprehension that haunts one night and day. It's just free-floating fear, a sense of great and imminent doom that can't be reasoned away. Feeling anxious over a bill, or a relationship, or a work issue now and then doesn't begin to approximate the pervasive distress of chronic anxiety. An occasional shadow crossing the sun is not a raging storm.

Clinical anxiety isn't just a figment of an overactive imagination. Cold hard science proves its existence. For example, it's clearly genetic: A child is six times more likely to have it if one of his parents does. Yet despite the evidence to the contrary, we still consider anxiety to be a character defect, a moral failing that could be cured if a person just showed a little more grit.

Take my friend who doesn't like being around my anxiety. He says it disturbs him to listen to me talk about it. I can hear our canceled lunch conversation now:

"You're acting funny," he'd say. "What's going on?"

"I'm terrified I'm going to end up alone," I'd say.

"You're not alone at the moment, you're with me," he'd say. "Stop worrying about the future."

"But what if I'm right?"

"But what if you're wrong?"

"But what if I'm right?"

I'd feel his patience unraveling. "Why are you obsessing about this?" he'd say. "Order something, already."

"But isn't it better to worry now than to be blindsided later?"

"You could be hit by a meteorite later. Why don't you worry about that?"

"Why? Do you know something?" I'd ask, scanning the sky.

He'd sigh. "You're wearing me out."

Now this may be strictly a personal take, but as with depression, I don't want to be talked out of my feelings. I want to enumerate, out loud, all the reasons why I know something wicked is coming my way and is about to feast on my bones. It helps to get those thoughts out of my head—even I can sometimes hear how absurd they sound when they're exposed to the open air.

But the way we treat anxiety these days, you're not allowed to dwell on those "dangerous" thoughts. You have to medicate them away, disprove them via cognitive therapy, or otherwise pretend that they don't exist; which makes for a very lonely, very guilty mind when they refuse to leave. So maybe it's best that my friend said no to our lunch—I'd feel so isolated in his company. Trust in science and logic, he'd tell me. Two and two will always make four, and prime numbers will go on forever. If I could just believe this strongly enough, there'd be no reason to worry. To him, life is that explicable.

But reason and logic are generally useless and frankly, potentially harmful tools when it comes to handling my anxiety. They dismiss and belittle and can make things worse. That's why I'd feel much calmer and happier if my physics-spouting friend would just sit there and let me tell him I'm scared. I wouldn't feel so completely alone, and maybe he wouldn't feel so puzzled and impatient. He'd know why I seem irrational and on edge, and we could both investigate the underpinnings of my concern. Maybe, who knows, it would dissipate—maybe even in laughter. At the very least, I would feel heard; nothing soothes the frenzy of anxiety like being heard, and being loved and accepted anyway.

— — —

THE RULES OF SUICIDE

Camus said it best: "There is but one truly serious philosophical problem, and that is suicide. Judging whether life is or is not worth living amounts to answering the fundamental question of philosophy."

Fundamental philosophy aside, I've learned a lot about suicide over the years. Some of the knowledge comes from straight research, but mostly I know way too much about suicide because of my own attempts. I've met that enemy face-to-face; I've studied his features up close. Unfortunately, my reluctant insight also comes from having lost people I love to suicide. Every time it happens, I think I've steeled myself against the grief. But I haven't, and I doubt I ever will. That's why I want to share what I've learned, however ruthless the lessons may seem. It's essential knowledge, cruelly acquired.

First, a note of reassurance: in my opinion, assigning blame after a suicide is pointless. There are always echoes of guilt: Could I have said something, done something, seen it coming? If only I'd been there at that last moment. If only we hadn't had that stupid fight. If only I'd seen the signs. The "if onlys" ring in your head so loudly, they drown out everything else. This may be small comfort to offer, but I think it's best to let go of the guilt. I know from my own experience that sometimes, at my lowest, nothing anyone can say or do will deter me.

But there are a few proactive things to try with those who are still alive and willing (however reluctantly) to listen. As is always the case with mental illness, preemptive education is key. Learning the nasty truths about suicide, and imparting those truths to someone in distress, can be an extremely powerful intervention. It may seem harsh, and it may not be what that person wants to hear at that moment, but you might just shock him into wanting to live. Here are three hard facts about suicide that have made a huge difference to me:

1. PEOPLE WILL BE VERY ANGRY AT YOU IF YOU MAKE AN ATTEMPT

It doesn't matter that you're suffering so much you feel you have to resort to a step this drastic. Suicide is and always has been the ultimate social taboo. People are terrified of it and therefore terrified of you for not having honored the rules. At a time when you need tremendous love and support, you will be yelled at, cursed, accused of cowardice and selfishness, abandoned, and generally made to feel like a pariah. This is a guarantee.

Rather than celebrating your survival, people will think you weren't serious. They will underestimate your pain. How many times have I heard those terrible words: "It must have just been a cry for help." Now when you tell people you feel suicidal, they will think you're crying wolf. You will lose all credibility with your loved ones and your doctors, just when you need it the most.

2. YOUR DOCTORS MAY REFUSE TO TREAT YOU

Many of us, when we enter therapy, make a contract promising we will not attempt suicide for the duration of treatment. Believe me, doctors will enforce that promise. I once had a caring, committed psychiatrist call me in the hospital after I'd made a serious attempt. I ran to the phone, eager for his help. He terminated our relationship, not without empathy but with no wiggle room, either. Even if you've never entered such a contract, you're likely to experience problems with your current and future treatment. Doctors are very concerned about their liability, which means it might also be difficult for you to find another health care professional who's willing to take you on. You're now officially labeled a risk.

3. YOU RUN A HUGE RISK OF MAIMING YOURSELF

The body revolts. It clings to life, no matter how ardently you try to break that bond. But just because you don't manage to die doesn't mean that you escape suffering. Time and again, I've inflicted horrible injuries on myself while spiraling into unconsciousness. I once fell so badly after an overdose, I couldn't walk for six months without the use of crutches. Another time, I sustained such terrible bruises all over my body that when I was taken to the emergency room, the police assumed I was a victim of domestic assault and hauled my boyfriend in for questioning. That was the end of that relationship. However you may feel about life right now, it's a mighty and tenacious force that we apparently are not supposed to tamper with.

I'd tattoo these grim but inescapable facts on your loved one's brain—or better yet, write them down and post them on his refrigerator because the brain isn't always accessible when someone's suicidal. And you need to remind him of some softer truths, too: (1) You love him, no matter what; and (2) Life is constantly changing. Not so very long ago, I was practicing knots for a noose. Today I'm sitting in a charming outdoor café at a museum, eating asparagus purée soup with a grilled-cheese sandwich. What changed in my life? Nothing—except my brain chemistry. Today, the grilled cheese tastes delicious.

RANDOM ACTS OF KINDNESS

Several summers ago, I was struggling financially, and as a result of the stress, I developed an ulcer. Then I found out I had cancer on my nose and needed reconstructive surgery. But the worst was yet to come: the man I loved left me—without a word, without any warning. This combination of events proved too much for me, and I dive-bombed into a vicious, suicidal depression. All I'd ever known boiled down to this: if the world could be so heartless and cruel, I didn't want to be a part of it anymore.

My support team did what they could—my therapist phoned me every day, my psychopharmacologist prescribed drug after endless drug. But I was so shocked by the savagery of the universe, I couldn't understand why anyone who loved me wouldn't just let me die. I didn't know then that life doesn't care if you're suicidal. The gas bill needs to be paid regardless; the body still needs to be fed.

That summer, in my writing group, I casually wrote about a situation I was facing: I could afford either groceries or medication, but not both. I didn't write this seeking help, I was just cataloging a realistic, if gruesome, fact of my life. A couple of days later I received a card in the mail from my group, with a check large enough to get me past my dilemma. I didn't have the slightest idea what to do—I was stunned and perplexed and deeply touched. I wasn't sure what the proper protocol was for taking money from friends. But desperation trumps protocol every time, and I quickly cashed the check.

A few weeks later there was a knock at my door. I opened it to a delivery man bearing a glorious bunch of white lilies. They were from a person who knew I was severely depressed because I kept canceling our lunch plans. Getting flowers is always great, but these were extraordinary because there was no special occasion, and they were a custom bouquet. The sender knew from reading *Manic* that white lilies mean the world to me. Every day I inhaled that heavenly fragrance, I felt a little farther from death.

Shortly after that I ran into a man I hadn't seen in years. He asked me how I was, and I didn't have the energy to edit.

"I feel awful," I said. "Life sucks."

"I know," he said. "Me, too."

With that we cut clean through the viscera and got down to the heart of things. I told him about my faithless lover. It turned out his wife had left him, too.

"I don't see any point in going on," I said. "I'll never love again."

"You may love, but it will never be the same," he responded.

All this on the street corner. You'd think it would have increased my despondency to have my worst suspicions about life confirmed, but it didn't. It made me feel human again to be privy to another person's wounds. They were different from mine, but close enough to make me realize that I didn't have a monopoly on pain. The music was sad, but it struck a universal chord.

By unspoken consensus we walked to a nearby park and spent the next two hours commiserating. I got to say everything I wanted and someone listened and gave a damn. And I listened back with an intensity of empathy that surprised me—I'd thought that part of me was dead. As the day slipped tranquilly into night, I could feel something ripped and shredded inside me slowly begin to knit together.

Money, flowers, and an open ear: random acts of kindness performed not for gain or advantage, but simply because someone cared enough to make the effort. It made me realize an essential truth. The world may be brutal at times, but it's also capable of great compassion, and that's a world I want to live in. I'll never again underestimate the boundless power of a small benevolence. I know now what that transaction's worth—you not only get to reap the karma, you may just rewrite a life.

I'M NOT SICK AND YOU
CAN'T MAKE ME

When I was a litigation attorney, I had to learn to think fast on my feet. Courts are no place to dither; judges have zero tolerance for hesitation. As a result, I can usually improvise my way through question-and-answer sessions at readings and lectures. It helps that growing older has made me humbler than I used to be. I can now say, "I'm sorry, I don't know the answer to that" without dissolving into a puddle of shame. But there's one question that I consider my nemesis, the one I most dread to hear, and that always—always!— gets asked: "How do you help someone who doesn't want help?"

The question is inevitably preceded by a very sad story about a loved one's continuing fall from grace; the devastating impact it's having on all those around him; and his inexplicable refusal to take medication, go to therapy, or even acknowledge that anything is wrong. I can tell who's going to ask the question almost before they speak: Frustration is written across their faces. They are maxed out: they've tried everything—and yet they're hoping against hope that I'll have an answer.

I wish to God I did. I wish I could provide the magic words that would instantly deliver a happy ending. Instead, I've learned to come clean. "You know what?" I say. "That's the hardest question I'm ever asked, and it breaks my heart every time I hear it. I don't have an answer, but I have some suggestions."

Then I tell them about the National Alliance on Mental Illness (nami.org) and the International Bipolar Foundation (ibpf.org), both terrific organizations for families and friends of loved ones with mental illness. When that response feels too clinical, I share my personal thoughts about this problem:

1. First and most obvious (clichés exist for a reason), always remember the airplane scenario. When the oxygen mask drops, you have to put on your own before assisting anyone else. It makes total sense: When you can't breathe, you can't help. But so many of us forget this in crisis, when others are screaming loud in our ears. We let our own needs dangle, unattended, while we try to solve other people's lives. The result: nobody survives. The harsh reality is, dealing with someone in denial can be exhausting. You've got to take care of yourself first, or you're no good to anyone else.

2. Recognize the tremendous fear that lies beneath a refusal to seek help. In most cases I can almost guarantee that the person knows, at some repressed level, that something is wrong with him. His life is becoming unmanageable, to borrow twelve-step wisdom. But he doesn't dare lift his head above ground for fear of what he might see—and the even greater fear that there will be no way out.

3. Know about "anosognosia." It's a big word, with a big meaning. People who suffer from anosognosia aren't simply in denial about their illness; they don't even realize they're ill. Anosognosia means lack of insight or awareness, and it's most common in individuals with schizophrenia and schizoaffective disorder, although it's not limited to them. Doctors have determined that in many cases, actual changes to the brain structure may be the cause. I bring it to your attention—and to the attention of as many law enforcement personnel as I can—because I think it might engender a better understanding of why some mentally ill people just don't seem to get it. Maybe they can't.

4. Acknowledge what you share with the person in denial, however disparate your situations may seem on the surface. After all, we all use denial as a defense mechanism from

time to time. How else could we face the great unsolvable mystery that is life? Realizing you have some common ground may lessen the agonizing bewilderment you feel when you look at the other person.

This last point, subtle as it may sound, has made all the difference in the world to me. For years, I was one of those intransigent people who refused to admit to myself or others that I needed help. When I finally acknowledged that I was in trouble, I didn't suddenly become more lovable or easier to fix—I was just easier to understand. I wasn't an enigma anymore, a problem that couldn't and wouldn't be solved. I was human, fallible, and therefore just like the people who were trying to help me. Bridges slowly began to be built; the great divide grew narrower at last. It taught me an essential lesson, which is all I can pass on to others now: empathy reaches where sympathy can't.

SECTION V

Troubleshooting

BAD COPING SKILLS

"I have not failed. I've just found
10,000 ways that won't work."
—Thomas A. Edison (1847–1931)

— — —

Virginia Satir, a prominent clinical therapist, nailed the dilemma: "Problems are not the problem," she said. "Coping is the problem." People respond to stressful experiences in both adaptive (helpful) and maladaptive (harmful) ways. Unfortunately, maladaptive coping methods—such as denial, avoidance, substance abuse, self-harm, rumination, social withdrawal, to name just a few—can actually be effective in reducing immediate symptoms of anxiety and distress. But their end result is only to increase dysfunction because the core problem is never dealt with, only whisked away for a short while. Ultimately, they simply perpetuate the pain, creating new and sometimes even more intractable problems on top of the old.

Researchers agree that it's very common for a person to use more than one maladaptive coping method. Where they differ, however, is on how these harmful strategies develop.

Some believe they arise instinctually, from our subconscious. But child development experts believe they are a result of toxic early environments—invalidating interactions with caregivers, as well as a lack of healthy alternatives and exposure to uncontrollable stress (https://www.ncbi.nlm.nih.gov/pmc/articles/PMC4442090/).

How they begin seems less important than how to end them. Naturally, being introduced to healthier coping alternatives is essential, and this is one of the ways that therapy can transform a life. But it's also critical to recognize the purpose the maladaptive behavior is serving—what exactly is the seminal problem that's being avoided? Otherwise we risk simply replacing it with another, perhaps even more harmful, avoidant behavior. Again, it's hard work that can be achieved in a therapeutic setting.

The good news is that brain plasticity isn't just a theory—it's proven science. Learning new and more effective ways to cope with stress will actually lay new neural pathways that can prevent further damage and even reclaim a life.

GOING UNDERGROUND: ISOLATING

I heard it before I felt it: a long screech of brakes, protesting their inability to stop, helpless against the inevitable. Then that horrible sound, unlike any other, of metal crunching metal. I went blank as I realized it was my car under assault, that it was me being catapulted against the unyielding seat belt. Fortunately, I walked away from the accident, but my poor car could only limp its way onto a tow truck. What might have seemed like a lucky break turned into a nightmare, as intransigent insurance companies and scheming body shops and words like "totaled" were thrown into the mix.

I was distraught and distressed and all kinds of upset. But I'm relatively good at facing situational depressions like this—the kind that arrive in response to some external calamity. They can be extremely anxiety-provoking at the moment, but they usually yield to time and good therapy. And clearly, this was a rotten situation, which would have upset anyone. So I turned to my friends for sympathy and advice, and they were forthcoming. Everyone's had a car accident. They all understood what I was going through.

A week passed, and the initial shock began to dissipate. But inexplicably, I felt worse. I sought out my friends again, and once again they came through. "It's perfectly normal," one of them said. "Reality is starting to set in now."

Well, reality kept on setting in, deeper and deeper with each passing day. I felt like I had when those brakes started squealing—I knew something really bad was about to happen, but I couldn't get out of the way. I wondered if I was getting the flu. My body was achy and sluggish, my head so heavy it was hard to lift it even to watch TV. I felt pathetic, unlovable, a total wreck—as damaged as my mangled car and just as unworthy of repair.

I reached out to my friends yet again. The responses were much slower this time around. The general gist of them was, "Sorry you still feel so bad." That "still" stood out; it could have been in all caps. I was trying people's patience now.

It happens sometimes—situational depressions turn into major chemical depressions. Then I'm no longer fighting external events, I'm waging war with my own mind. What was once sympathetic to the outside world seems neurotic and obsessive. Friends are no longer a resource, they're the enemy because they don't or can't understand my pain. It's happened to me time and again: in spite of all my years in therapy, my rigorous compliance with medication, the advice I've given and taken to heart, I succumb. I forget all my carefully honed coping skills and fall back on the same old habit that has served me, badly, for as far back as I can remember.

I go underground.

I don't want help from anyone then, from doctors or friends or any other well-meaning persons. I simply want to be alone. With a vehemence I can hardly describe, I can't stand the thought of anyone trying to soothe me. The prospect of a hug is anathema—I can't bear to be touched, not for even a second. The stimulation would short-circuit my already overloaded nerves. So I erect a prickly, thorn-strewn wall between me and any possible resources.

Alone feels safe; it asks nothing of me. It's a haven of silence, into which I can pour all the wretched thoughts and feelings I can't expose to the rest of the world without risking rejection. Alone is that rare space without stigma, where I can be my true self. I don't have to smile, or talk, or pretend to be interested in anything else. My tears can fall freely, and no one is around to try to stop them. I can wipe them away with my old flannel pj's, and not feel ashamed of those, either.

The problem with isolating is that being alone with my thoughts only makes me think harder. Why, when I most need the comfort of others, do I adamantly refuse to be held? Why do I shrink from the extended hand, which might be just what I need at the moment? Obviously, the best thing I can do for myself during a chemical depression is to engage, to seek help, to take that one small step outside my comfort zone. But the urge to be alone is just too strong to resist.

I'm not sure why I feel so guilty about this; after all, I didn't invent isolation. No doubt there was a suffering caveman somewhere, who likewise sought shelter away from his tribe. It may be human nature to bond, but it's also natural to want to slip away to lick your wounds in private. In fact, it's extremely common for depressed individuals to isolate as a coping mechanism, despite the health risks clearly associated with it. (One study claims lack of social connection is comparable to smoking fifteen cigarettes a day.) That doesn't help me change my behavior, but it does reduce the shame somewhat. I feel childishly justified: if so many other people can do it, then so can I. I'm shut off in my own little world, but in truth I'm never really alone. I'm in the company of thousands of strangers, all doing what we shouldn't.

BAD BEDTIME STORIES:
SELF-BLAME

Years ago I was hospitalized at Cedars-Sinai after a suicide attempt. I wasn't very happy about it at the time—I didn't like the people, didn't like the program, and especially didn't like the doctor who'd been assigned to me. "You don't handle stress very well," she told me in our first session, as if that could somehow sum up everything that was wrong with me and shock me into new behavior. It didn't. I felt aggrieved and insulted and went into hiding in the open air. I withdrew from any help she might have given me. Her statement still rankles, after all this time.

Years later, I sat in another doctor's office, clutching an emesis bowl the nurse had given me. I'd been violently sick for several months, and this was my third attempt to find a doctor who could tell me why it wouldn't stop, and what was going on with my body.

"Sounds like an ulcer," the doctor said. "You must not handle stress very well."

I was catapulted back to Cedars-Sinai and the anger and guilt I'd felt at that time. I thought I'd evolved past it, that I was an old hand at dealing with stigmatic illness. After all, I'd been diagnosed with bipolar disorder over twenty years before. As time passed and the illness didn't succeed in killing me, I thought it only made me stronger, better able to handle the rigors of life. I thought I held my head up just a little higher than most because I had sunk as low as suicide and yet, somehow, survived.

So when my doctor said "ulcer," I visibly cringed. Ulcers happen to dissolute advertising execs like those East Coast guys on *Mad Men*, who drink too much and attack life too vigorously. But I've been sober for over twenty years, and I'm not a typical Type-A anymore. I chose to leave the practice of law to pursue a cleaner, quieter existence: to write, to reflect, to observe.

But apparently, I still "didn't handle stress very well." The shame of that phrase spun around and around in my head until I finally realized that the greatest stressor of all wasn't my ulcer, or even my bipolar disorder. It was the story I told myself about myself, the words I elected to use, the truths I chose to believe. My relationship with stress was mine to define, and I wasn't defining it very well.

Self-stigma is every bit as pernicious as the stigma one encounters in the outside world; maybe even worse because we know ourselves so well we know exactly which buttons to push. It's too easy to believe in my own bedtime stories—those terrible things I tell myself when I can't get to sleep: you're hopeless, you're weak, you can't handle stress. Old words, familiar but worn to shreds. *Was it possible*, I wondered, *to tell myself a different tale—one with a happier ending?*

Well, yes and no. It's hard to let go of your most cherished beliefs, even the ones that are torturing you. But one bleak night when my thoughts kept betraying me, I took a deep breath and tried out a new beginning: "You're telling me I can't handle stress? Are you kidding? I've battled mental illness all my life. I've been subjected to more medication trials than a lab rat. And I'm still here as Exhibit A." The words were not just plausible; they went down like warm milk.

Balm, you would think, to any ulcer; that night I did sleep better. But then came the harsh light of a new morning and damn it, the dawn of more doubts. I couldn't help but think that the doctors knew something about me that I didn't know—that their exams and their instruments verified a fault that somehow proved their theory, that I was sick because I simply couldn't handle stress.

I knew in my heart that this wasn't true, and that I'd work through its fallacy yet again. But this is what self-blame does: It eats through your faith in yourself like a poison. It burns until it's all you can feel and all you can believe. It's arsenic, laced with a little truth.

— — —

THE WEB: OBSESSION

I don't like to admit that I'm obsessive, despite how often I hear it from others. I prefer to think that I'm highly focused. Driven. Single-minded. But every now and then, even I have to acknowledge that I've gone over to the dark side, where reason doesn't shine.

Like with spiders. I loathe spiders. Nasty, creepy, primeval things, with the emphasis on "evil." They're out to get me, I just know it. So when I was driving my car the other day and saw an enormous spider climbing on my side view mirror, I swerved all the way into the other lane, narrowly missing a FedEx truck.

My window was closed; I was in no immediate danger of being attacked. The only real danger I faced was that I couldn't stop staring at the spider as he clung to the mirror, all eight legs spread-eagled across the glass. Several horns honked at me as I lurched from side to side, trying to knock him off. No luck. Revulsion gradually gave way to wonder: *how was he holding on?*

I knew of a street nearby where there was never any traffic, and cops would be unlikely to lurk. It was me against the spider now, and battle needs a clear playing field. I headed there and floored it: forty, forty-five, fifty. I spun a U-turn in the middle of the road and came screeching to a halt. I looked at the mirror, and hooray! No spider.

Feeling triumphant and clever, I resumed my trip at a more leisurely speed. Approaching Sunset Boulevard, I flicked on my left turn signal, dutifully glanced at my side view mirror—and there it was, a single crooked leg pawing at the glass, followed by another, then another, then another, and so forth, until the damned thing had crawled its way back home.

I shuddered, but I had to admire its tenacity. It was obsessed with this particular mirror and refused to be evicted. Maybe obsession wasn't as bad a character trait as I had always thought. Maybe if I gave my own obsessions freer reign, I could accomplish marvelous things, like this spider had in the face of great odds.

Okay, what the hell—I decided I would give myself an entire day to be as obsessive as I liked. I wouldn't try to fight it, I'd just give in. I'd take my psyche off its interminable leash and let it cling or not cling, attach or detach, whatever mind games it wanted to play. For once, I wouldn't worry about how much I was worrying.

So I flitted through the myriad of possible things to obsess about, and quickly settled on the least productive one: men. One man in particular, who had called me yesterday and vaguely mentioned something about dinner tonight. It was three-thirty and I still hadn't heard from him. Should I go ahead and eat something? Should I make other plans? And what about getting dressed? Dressing for dinner—especially a dinner date—at the very least meant curling my eyelashes and finding the right lingerie and picking out killer shoes. That took time; how much time did I have?

Before long, annoyance turned into angst. Why couldn't I find a man who cared enough about me to commit to a single evening? I was an afterthought, a maybe if, a rung below essential. I seized the pain and wrung it dry. What was wrong with me anyway, that I still had to fret about dinner dates? Was it because I was bipolar? Was that always going to get in my way? Would there never be a cure?

I turned onto my street, my eyes obscured by tears. I parked my car and stepped out. The spider was still sitting there, obviously in love with its reflection in the mirror. I whacked it hard with my purse. *Obsession can be a dangerous thing*, I thought. Best not to indulge it.

— — —

BLAME IT ON BASIC INSTINCT: IMPULSIVITY

Like most attorneys, I know how to bend the law, but I'm essentially a law-abiding citizen. I'm the least likely person to be profiled as a problem: I'm middle-class, white, well kempt and well behaved. That is, when I'm not manic.

One Saturday night in the early '90s, I went to catch a movie at the Third Street Promenade, an upscale outdoor shopping mecca in Santa Monica. The breeze from the ocean was chilly, and even though I was trying to stop drinking—alcohol did strange things to me—I figured an Irish coffee would warm me up just fine. Which it did, and the second and third one chased the chill away even further.

When I sauntered out of the pub, I surveyed the world and thought it was good. I had a promising career, a budding romance, and a full life spread out before me, just mine for the taking. I bought the movie ticket, pocketed it, and decided to stroll for the remaining twenty minutes. Well, stroll might not be the right word. The Promenade's always chaotic, but on a Saturday night it's positively frenetic, with jugglers and acrobats and rappers and the like, all hustling the tightly packed crowd.

I shuffled along with the rest of them, elbowing for space. As more and more people bumped into me, or I into them, the fine haze from my buzz began to disappear. I could feel that sharp nip in the air again, although the back of my neck was clammy with sweat. My heart thudded; I stopped and tried to take my pulse, but I kept getting jostled. Was I sick? No, but I felt dizzy and feverish, like I was sprinting even though I was standing still at the stoplight. I knew I ought to just leave and seek solace, away from the hubbub and clamor. But the whiskey said no, the party's not over. I wasn't conversant enough with my symptoms back then to realize what my body was trying to tell me: that my mood was rocketing straight up to mania, and the whiskey was just the chaser.

Then I heard it, in the midst of the mêlée: a single high, unwavering note, like the voice of an angel slicing straight through the babel. I pushed my way toward it, not caring how many toes I stepped on or how many packages I knocked out of arms. All the while, it hung there, waiting for me to find it. And finally, I did: It was coming from a beautiful young girl, maybe sixteen or seventeen, standing in a small carved-out space of her own. She wore threadbare jeans and sandals despite the cold, and there was a woven basket at her feet with a few bills and some change in it.

The girl was singing, a cappella, a song I've always loved: "Ave Maria." She sang in Latin, just the way I'd learned it from the nuns: "Ave Maria, gratia plena . . ." The noise and the tumult and my own inner cacophony disappeared. I closed my eyes and was transported back into the stillness of the nave, the dusky smell of incense, the hush of a hundred souls praying, and above it all the choirboys' pure "Ave, ave dominus, dominus tecum."

When she finished, I wanted to wail. Everything I'd told myself before was a lie. My life was not fine at all; it was buried in the bottom of a whiskey glass and I couldn't find it no matter how deeply I drank. In the space of a few seconds, just a few notes really, my mood had careened out of control and I was no longer the person in charge. I dumped all the money I had in my purse into the girl's basket, easily a couple hundred dollars, to make up for my sins. She smiled at me and I knew everything was going to be all right again, but then someone darted in from the crowd and snatched up the basket.

I saw him, a tall skinny kid wearing a Lakers cap. He zigged and zagged and I ran after him, screaming "Thief! Thief!" But no one heard or no one cared because the tide just kept flowing toward me and I was trapped and he was getting away. Then he tripped over a baby stroller, and I was about to catch up with him in the intersection when someone grabbed me by the arm and pulled me back onto the sidewalk. A cop.

"No, let me go, he's getting away," I shouted, and tugged myself free of his grip.

"The light's red, and you're not going anywhere," he said, snatching me back, both hands on my shoulders.

"But you don't understand, he stole all the money and you're in my way—" and then I lost sight of the boy. I spun around and let the cop have it.

"That poor girl, she doesn't even have proper shoes, and he stole all her money and you just stood there and let him get away, like a big fat stupid cow."

He flushed red, and pulled me closer. "What did you say?" he said. I repeated the insult, yelling to be heard over the din.

"Smells like someone's been drinking tonight," he said. "Let's see some I.D."

Maybe if I'd been in my right mind I would have pulled out my driver's license and apologized. But I was furious and beneath that, scared to death—drunk and disorderly in public might get me disciplined or even disbarred. Maybe if I cooperated, I'd get off easy, but all my instincts said, yeah right. So I shrugged off his meaty hands and made a motion as if to search through my purse. Then I turned tail and ran for my life.

I heard him shouting after me, and I was terrified. Resisting arrest, what do they give you for that? But I have to admit I was exhilarated, too. I melted like hot butter into the crowd, as if this was what I'd been meant to do all my life: evade the law, not enforce it. Like an animal, I knew exactly where I needed to go—I had to hide in the darkest hole I could find. And there it was, right in front of me.

A long line stretched out in front of the multiplex, but it meant nothing to me. When I'm manic, I never wait in line. I brazened my way up to the front, flashed my ticket, and ran to the very last theater in the back, where the cop would never find me. As the lights went down, I finally began to get calm, my heartbeat returning to normal. I'd always felt at home at the movies, safe in the anonymous dark. And I had to laugh at the irony: the film was *Basic Instinct*.

I sat through it twice, not venturing out until after midnight. The Promenade had quieted down, the shoppers and street performers gone. The cop was long gone, too, I hoped. But I took no chances—I dashed to my car. And I didn't return to the Promenade for years after that, until I was good and sober and could hear what my body was trying to tell me.

By then, honesty had caught up with me, and I wanted to make amends. Not to the cop—I wasn't evolved enough for that—but to the girl. I realized what had happened that night was as much my fault as the tall skinny kid's. If I hadn't made that grand, impulsive, manic gesture of tossing all my money away, the boy probably wouldn't have stolen her basket and she'd have headed tranquilly home that night, with her evening's wages safely in hand.

Whenever I've visited the Promenade since, I've listened for that angel's voice. But as often as I've looked for her, I've never found her again. Now I feel guilty whenever I hear my beloved "Ave Maria." There's no such thing as a clean escape. Not when you're manic. Not if you care.

▬ ▬ ▬

A WALKING WOUND:
REJECTION SENSITIVITY

I'd been working on a story for my writing group for an unusually long time, and I finally felt it was ready. Actually, I thought it was some of my best writing ever—all about love and loss and the rhapsody of desire. Deep stuff, embroidered by lyrical metaphors of which I was rather proud. I care deeply for the people in my group, and I wanted to reward their kindness to me with some beautiful words.

When I read the piece aloud I enunciated as clearly as possible, fully savoring each syllable as it left my lips. The room was very quiet: no coughs or twitching or yawns, which is usually a good sign for a writer. I felt triumphant when I reached the last line. I had that marvelous sensation of having picked out just the right gift for someone you love.

Except they didn't like it.

They didn't come right out and say that, but there was extended critique about a point I felt was totally irrelevant. I wanted to protest, "But you don't get it, I made that perfectly clear at the beginning, and here, and here, and there, and what you're suggesting would change the whole piece." But I kept quiet and jotted down some of the notes because when enough people disagree with you, it's time to take heed. Not that I thought they were right, but they had my attention and reluctant respect.

The whole event took maybe twenty minutes, although while it was happening it felt interminable. I looked forward to becoming anonymous again, for the spotlight to shine on someone else. But part of me dreaded it being over because I knew that was when my personal critique would start. Once I wasn't wearing my civilized public face anymore, my primitive insides would take over and I'd tear myself apart.

Like this: "You can't write. You never could. You're only deluding yourself. Look, these people are your dearest friends and even they don't like your story. Who are you fooling, trying to write? Stop it, you're only embarrassing yourself. Go sit in a corner and shut up."

Criticism and I have never made friends. It doesn't take much of it for me to lose my bearings, to feel lost in a tortuous maze of doubt. Although I know my reaction is intense and excessive, I also know I'm not alone in this. When I facilitated a support group at UCLA, time and again I'd watch the patients relentlessly focus on the smallest slights, which would send them spiraling down into depression and even suicidal despair. A word here, a look there, and suddenly the entire world turned malevolent.

I understood this with all my heart. I even understood it clinically. A psychiatrist once explained to me that a key symptom of bipolar disorder is "extreme rejection sensitivity." I remember wanting to hug him for those words. How lovely—a medical term that made sense of my life. I'd always thought my propensity to wound too easily was a fatal flaw in my makeup, a mortifying example of how weak and narcissistic and frail I truly am. I never imagined it was part of my diagnosis.

The solution to this hypersensitivity may be cocooned in time. I've repeatedly heard people say that as they grow older, they care less and less what others think of them. That makes the whole process of aging more tenable to me. I doubt that I'll ever feel happy when I don't get praise; I just hope I won't immediately start drafting my epitaph. I look forward to a day when I'm wizened and feisty enough not to give a damn anymore, to be able to hold on to my own opinion in spite of what other people say. All by myself, without any drugs: a white-haired whippersnapper, who knows what she knows. And writes what she wants. And it's fine.

— — —

THE VIRTUES OF BEING RUDE: BAD BORDERS

Outwardly, things felt safe enough. I was sitting in my favorite café, at my favorite table, writing or at least making plans to write. This is my nirvana spot: it's cozy, familiar, not really quiet but tolerable with ear plugs in. I'd just ordered my usual lunch—a cup of gazpacho with five-grain bread—when the man at the table next to me asked me what I was writing.

"A book," I said, hoping that was a vague enough answer to dissuade him from further small talk. It wasn't.

"What kind of book?" he asked.

I gave him the shorthand answer. "A memoir." I've found that a lot of people don't know what a memoir is, so rather than look ignorant they stop the conversation right there. It's worked often enough before.

"What's a memoir?" he said.

Great. A talker. Right next to me, so close our bodies would have touched if either had extended a hand. "It's a book about yourself," I said. Damn it, I knew what was coming next. I haven't found the right shut-up answer to that question yet, in spite of years of trying.

And sure enough: "So what have you done that makes you interesting enough to write about?"

This is where I usually get them to stop. I take out my big guns of discomfort and stigma and let them have it, full barrel: "I have bipolar disorder," I say. "I write about that."

But this guy wasn't deterred. "What's bipolar disorder?" he said.

Ah, come on. I gave him my stock answer. "It's a mental illness that causes extreme mood swings," I said.

The waitress came with my meal then, and I hoped that my feigned fervent interest in my food would signal my reluctance to talk further. Nope.

"I have mood swings," he said. "Everybody has mood swings. What makes you so special?"

Twelve little words were all I needed to reclaim my equanimity: "I'm sorry, but I need to get back to my writing now." But somehow, I couldn't say them. I was so irritable I was afraid I'd bark them out and hurt his feelings. Then I feared he'd retaliate against me somehow. I wasn't thinking this through at the time, but it's how I operate—I don't put up borders until it's way too late to make the attempt.

He badgered me throughout the rest of my meal, although perhaps I shouldn't say "badgered." Maybe he was just curious, and not very good at taking social cues. But I felt intensely observed the entire time: Every sip of soup was an ordeal, every bite of bread a challenge. I hate being watched while I eat, it makes me very self-conscious. And then I had to answer his persistent questions while trying to chew my food.

Finally, he left and I was alone with my opened computer and empty page. I was furious that I hadn't been more assertive. "You're always such a wimp," I told myself. "You should never go out in public." That was the moment I should have seen depression coming, and didn't. Instead of reaching for my keyboard, I reached for another slice of bread and the jar of heavenly hazelnut spread that comes with it. I've faced down this particular spread before—it's a true weakness of my flesh, and usually I avoid it like the plague. But that afternoon, instead of just paying the check or calling my therapist or texting a friend or doing any one of the myriad interventions possible, I went straight for the hazelnut spread.

I ate the whole bottle, spoonful by spoonful, feeling worse with each delicious bite. Even when I ran out of bread, I just kept shoveling it in. It's not like me to lose control of myself like this in public. Usually I wait until I get home. But my agitation was so intense, I felt like I'd die if I didn't stuff it down—like I was the verbal equivalent of an Uzi and was about to fire at the next poor soul who tried to talk to me.

When the jar was finally empty, I left. I felt miserable and bloated, and knew what was waiting at home for me: more binging, until I was so uncomfortably full and disgusted with myself I'd fall asleep. Then there would be the writhings of remorse, until the depression had finally run its course. All because I didn't know how to fight for my little corner of solitude to keep me sane.

I've vowed that the next time this happens—because it will, it happens to me all the time—I'll risk hurting the intruder's feelings and put up whatever fences I can, as fast as I can, to protect myself. Maybe this isn't an issue for other people, but I think for the acutely sensitive it's a true dilemma. A safe place is more than a luxury. We need our walls, even if they offend those trying to look in. It isn't rude. It's survival.

— — —

GOOD COPING SKILLS

"Life isn't about finding yourself. Life
is about creating yourself."
—George Bernard Shaw (1856–1950)

"Do what you can, with what you
have, where you are."
—Theodore Roosevelt (1858–1919)

— — —

The ability to soothe ourselves in the face of stress is more than just a handy technique. Some psychoanalysts see it as an art form, the most critical of all our psychic tools. It's a life skill that most people learn—or don't learn—from their parents. But of course, the learning need not stop there.

New tools for managing negative emotions are a hot topic in mental health at the moment, although much of the excitement revolves around skills that were developed long ago and are only now being rediscovered. Mindfulness, for example, or meditation, or self-compassion: these are ancient wisdoms, repackaged to look fresh and shiny.

Relatively recent practices like dialectical behavior therapy (DBT) are particularly successful with emotion regulation. Similarly, cognitive reframing and distraction techniques help manage stress, as does thought-stopping (in its simplest form, snap a rubber band on your wrist to divert yourself from ruminations or cravings. It works, even if you do get a bit bruised in the process).

Ultimately, adaptive tools that promote skills to cope with anxiety, increase a sense of control, and lead to reduced stress levels "may not only affect physiologic stress systems, but also restore damaged systems that could otherwise result in pathology and dysfunction." Researchers even believe that fostering these skills in at-risk youth may eventually help circumvent socioeconomic or racial mental health disparities (https://www.ncbi.nlm.nih.gov/pmc/articles/PMC4442090/).

If coping is an art form, we're all innate artists. Good coping means letting your best instincts inspire you—and being vigilant about listening to that angel on your shoulder.

A DOSE OF BEAUTY

I was standing in front of a Turner painting, which depicted a storm at sea. At least I thought that's what it depicted—it was a late Turner so it was pretty abstract, and there were too many people in front of the curator's card for me to read the title. For a moment I was fidgety, wishing I were all alone in the museum and knew exactly what I was seeing. But then I thought, *did it really matter?* I liked getting lost in the sensuous swirl of textures and colors, all merging and melting into each other. Whatever it was, it was lovely.

That's exactly how I felt about my bipolar disorder at that moment. I knew it was doing strange things to my brain—but whatever it was, it was lovely. I suspected that what I was feeling right then wasn't what the other people around me were feeling. They weren't tasting that particular shade of saturated blue; that lonesome patch of yellow green in the corner—a lost ship, perhaps—didn't make them want to cry. I doubt they were inside the painting like I was, intensely aware of every brushstroke, every seemingly random smudge of impasto. They may have had the advantage of knowing what they were seeing, but they didn't know what it was like to swallow it whole.

Art has redeemed me; it's made me want to live. I can't count the number of times I've woken up in the morning determined to kill myself, then gone to a museum or gallery instead and forgotten all about it. I sometimes think if I'd grown up in a cultural mecca like New York City or Washington, DC, my life would have had a completely different trajectory. I'd be saner, or at least I'd have a safe haven for my intensity. Whenever my illness overwhelmed me, I'd just go take a hit of beauty.

But I'm fortunate enough. If I really need art, the Hammer Museum near UCLA is only a few minutes away. The permanent collection is small, but should speak volumes to anyone who's bipolar. It boasts two very disparate van Goghs: one of a bleak and dreary rectory garden in winter, all somber browns and grays. The other he painted at the end of his life, in the asylum at Saint-Rémy. It's the van Gogh style most people know and love: bold, vibrant colors and flame-like strokes, the trees so alive they seem to be dancing.

Ever since I first laid eyes on these two paintings, I had a mission: to see them hung together. For some ridiculous reason, they were always placed at opposite ends of the gallery. I wrote letters, made phone calls, and pestered the staff whenever I visited. Maybe somebody heard me, or maybe somebody finally just got it; because the last time I was there, the paintings were hung side by side. Seen separately, you'd think they were by two different artists, the moods and the execution are that far apart. But seen together, they're a portrait of the astonishing schism of which one soul is capable: manic depression incarnate.

I seriously doubt whether van Gogh could ever have witnessed the waltz in those trees, or captured the ache in that wintry garden, if he hadn't been bipolar. It's a cursed gift, and all of us who are drawn this way should appreciate this. It makes me suicidal, yes; it also gives me an exquisite sensitivity. My depressions force me to look at the world as it really is, so I'm privy to truth, however stark it may be. But mania lets me see past truth and into possibility— like the frenzy in a sunflower, or the white-hot brilliance of a starry night.

Staring into the Turner in that crowded museum, I realized I knew things other people couldn't. That used to make me feel alone. Sometimes it still does. But at that moment, breathing in the light and the paint and the colors, I only felt alive.

WHY NOT TRY THE TRUTH?

I have a friend who's a rock star—a genuine rock star, I kid you not. I cherish him, not just for his amazing talent and the fact that he has groupies, but for himself and the very down-to-earth humanity he exhibits when he's not performing onstage. So when I got his message about an upcoming show, I eagerly jotted down the date and cleared my schedule so I could go. I knew he was breaking in a new act, and I wanted to be there to support him, the way he's unfailingly been there for all my readings. But I didn't reckon on depression showing up for such an extended visit.

Sometimes, if I push myself really hard, I can function when I'm depressed. I can at least show up and pretend to be human, which is what I wanted to do for my friend: just be there for the body count. Who would see me, after all, with the spotlight trained on him? I wouldn't even have to speak, since no one could hear me over the din.

But that, unfortunately, was the problem. This wasn't a chamber music concert; this was Celtic punk rock and all that entailed: the incessant shouting, the amped-up atmosphere. People pushing past you, spilling their drinks, jostling to get a better view. There's a very fine but definite line in depression where sensory stimulation turns into torture. Light sears your eyes, touch burns your skin, and music morphs into raucous noise.

And then there would be that awful expectation of gaiety, the crushing pressure to have a good time. I tried to imagine myself in the crowd, grim-eyed amidst all the lit-up faces. I couldn't dance, I couldn't even move. I'd be a black hole, sucking the life out of the party. Or worse yet, what if I went and I lost control? If I started screaming to be heard, would I ever stop?

But—and it was a major but—I'd already said I would go, and canceling held its own terrors. I've learned the hard way that when I'm depressed, it can be extremely dangerous to call off my plans. It makes me feel like a flake and a fraud when I don't show up as promised. Which leaves me feeling even more depressed, which leads to yet more cancellations, until inevitably I'm left wallowing in self-hatred and isolation. And as every one of us who struggles with mental illness knows, isolation is suicide's favorite haunt.

So I couldn't go, but I couldn't not go, either.

My illness seemed to hold all the cards—until I remembered the ace I still held up my sleeve: maybe I could just be honest. Because it's not the canceling per se that does the harm, it's all the lying about it. Pretending that I have the Hong Kong flu, or my tire exploded, or my dog has rabies, whatever. All the elaborate excuses and scenarios I come up with to hide what's really happening—which is that I'm simply too heartsick to come out and play.

I had to force myself to sit down at my computer, but I finally sent my friend a brief message the morning of the concert, saying I was sorry but couldn't come because I was too depressed. He immediately wrote back, sending "lots of love." I knew that he would understand, but more important, I knew that I could forgive myself because I'd told the truth. We all get sick now and then.

— — —

THANKS, I'LL HAVE THE USUAL

A few weekends ago I showed up as usual at the Barnes & Noble bookstore where I research, hang out with other writers, and maybe get a little writing done, too. I could already taste the warm oatmeal cookie I always order with my latte. I was so eager to get inside I didn't even notice that the front door was securely padlocked. Without a word of warning, the Barnes & Noble was no more. It meant a lot more to me than losing yet another bookstore, which L.A. can scarcely afford. It meant losing the basic framework of my weekends. What would I do now, where would I go, and how could I work without my gang, my routine, and my cookie to sustain me?

I hate change.

This could easily be a cliché—nobody likes change—unless you understand the peculiar workings of my personal world. My internal landscape is always in flux, so I have no idea what the emotional weather will be when I wake up tomorrow. Gray and gloomy, with scudding storm clouds? Or so vividly, piercingly bright I have to squint to take it all in? I need some measure of outward stability to compensate for this unsettling inner lability.

And so, I want my regular waiter to greet me with "The usual?" when I show up at my favorite café (same order every time: gazpacho). I want Mondays to be yoga; Tuesdays to be therapy; Wednesdays to be my writing group; Thursdays to be the farmers' market (same order every time: white lilies)—and well, you get the drift. No substitutions; no exceptions.

I want stability in people, too. I resent it when my friends change their email addresses, let alone get remarried or find a new job. I'm not crazy about their aging, either—not because I don't empathize but because it makes them look and act differently. I want their faces to be, if not carved in stone, at least reliably etched in my memory.

With stability comes a hunger for order and an even deeper belief that if I just keep doing things the exact same way, in the exact same order, madness will have no hold on me. I realize this is pure magical thinking—superstitious at best, neurotic at worst. I know deep down that whether I relapse or not depends on a whole lot more than getting a dozen white lilies from one particular flower vendor every Thursday afternoon, or the perfect oatmeal cookie.

What really matters—and the only thing I should never change—is my personal sanity checklist. Every day without fail I must

1. Be vigilant about my symptoms;
2. Take my medication as prescribed;
3. Stay current on the medical research;
4. Reach out when I need to;
5. Give back when I can; and
6. Resist the temptation to lie in therapy.

These things lie squarely within my control and have nothing to do with forces beyond me, malevolent or otherwise. But still . . . Who can really say for sure? There must be some good reason for superstition, or we'd all be sashaying under ladders and blessing black cats. All I'm really certain of is that I'm incredibly lucky to be this functional, when so many others are not. And as long as I keep staying lucky, I intend to stick to what works whenever I can.

Am I predictable? Maybe. Boring? Perhaps. But ask any pro: batters hitting .300 should never alter their swings.

THE WORLD IN AN UPROAR: NOISE

It was a lovely dinner party: a dress-up affair, which was unusual in L.A. and fun for a change. Family silver graced the table, along with crisp linen napkins and gold-rimmed champagne flutes. Light jazz effervesced in the background. The other seven guests and I were in fine form, and conversation flowed. Life felt soothing and sophisticated, and I was right where I belonged.

Until I wasn't.

It started just after the cheese course, when the guests were well fed and well wined. Anecdotes gradually lengthened into stories, gestures got bigger, laughter grew louder. The man to the left of me set his glass down on the table, and it made a sharp clinking sound. Then the man to the right of me accidentally dropped his fork, and it clattered onto his plate. Across the table, a woman's charm bracelet jangled as she moved her hands. Small sounds, but I knew myself well enough to be worried: in the midst of the delightful conversation and music, all I heard were clinkings and clatterings and janglings, and little else that made any sense.

It escalated, until the voices sounded screechy, like a jaybird's. The jazz was a series of discordant riffs, and the laughter wasn't infectious; it was brassy and grating. The man next to me kept talking—not *to* me, but *at* me: a significant difference. I didn't even try to answer him, since I could barely hear what he was saying. All at once, a longing swept through me. I wanted to be elsewhere, quiet, home. What had started out as a lovely dinner had become nothing more than a terrible din.

It's not the first time that sound has turned the tables on me, intensifying from scarcely noticeable to almost unendurable in the space of a few moments. In fact, it's happened so often I actually researched it. It turns out there's a phenomenon called hyperacusis: an unusually low tolerance to ordinary sounds, the kind which don't bother most people. Anxiety plays a role in hyperacusis, and bipolar individuals may be particularly susceptible, given their heightened sensitivity overall. It's especially prevalent in mania, which doesn't surprise me: all my senses are on hyperdrive then.

But I wasn't manic that evening. And I was armed with information, even a technical term for what was going on with me, which usually makes a difference. So what was I supposed to do? Excuse myself from the dinner table, telling the hostess, "I'm sorry, but I feel my hyperacusis coming on?"

Once again, I struggled with an all-too-familiar demon: just because I'm different from other people, should I excuse myself from life?

It's never an easy question, especially in the midst of cacophony. So I did what I always do when social situations threaten to get the better of me: I escaped to the ladies' room. The guest bathroom was, not surprisingly, beautifully appointed and a genuine refuge. When I closed the door behind me, the noise fell away. I ran cool water over my wrists and fingers, and dabbed some perfume on my neck. Gradually, the buzzing in my ears became a low drone, and I was able to think again.

I reviewed the facts: (1) The hyperacusis was real; (2) The bipolar disorder was real. Together, they created what some poetic scientist has called "a collapsed tolerance for stimulation." *Reasonable grounds to isolate*, I thought; no one could blame me if I just said to hell with it and went home. No one, that is, but myself. I would know that I'd given up without a genuine fight. So I refreshed my lipstick and my courage, and emerged ready for battle.

The noise hit me again, like a shimmering wave of heat. Only this time I was ready for it, and I had a plan of action. The noisier it got, the less I would struggle. I'd allow the sounds to move past but not through me: I'd observe the scene without being a player. Lonely? Yes, but how much lonelier it would be if I insisted on my illness; if I allowed it to be the measure of me, and surrendered without even trying.

I sat down and smiled at the man on my left, then at the man on my right. I smiled at the woman across from me. I tried hard not to blame them for being so loud: no doubt there are reasons people find comfort in overwrought sound. Maybe they were shy, and the clamor relieved them of the need for reciprocal conversation. Maybe they felt ill-informed and were afraid to say things that might actually be heard. In short, maybe the noise was overcompensation for their own shortcomings rather than an intentional assault on my fragile nerves.

It's amazing how much simpler life can be when you refuse to take it personally.

I managed to make it through dessert, and even waited for another guest to leave before I skedaddled out of there. I was proud of myself for sticking it out and taking care of myself, but I knew it hadn't changed my essential antipathy to too much noise and stimulation—or my frustration that the rest of the world doesn't seem to feel the same way. Quite the opposite. Go to any popular restaurant, and just try to make yourself heard. Or take a walk down any city street, and try to escape the intimate details of everyone's cellular life. Tell me: Why do we shout at invisible people? To drown out the specter of silence, perhaps, because in silence you can only hear yourself—and heaven forbid, anything but that.

Is it really so strange to want library quiet, even though libraries are becoming anachronisms? When did we collectively forget the exquisite, shivery joy of a whisper? I can't help but wonder how much of my sensitivity is pathological, and how much is my sanity poking through.

— — —

SCHEDULING SANITY

For five days going on forever, I was trapped in my house with a contagious strep throat. I'd say I was slowly going insane, but when you're bipolar you have to use words like "insane" judiciously. So for five days I was alone with the TV, some books I'd been meaning to read, and my thoughts. The first day I figured, how great! I'll rest and catch up on my reading, maybe binge-watch for a while. Five days later, I'd finished the books, binged until I was thoroughly bored, and eaten my way through my provisions. I hadn't meant to eat so much, but boredom makes even sardines look appealing.

Enforced isolation isn't good for me. It's probably not good for anyone, but in my case it's particularly nerve-wracking, even dangerous. It means I'm living alone in my head, and my head is a cacophonous place. Usually I manage to silence my thoughts by suffocating them with action. Each week I aspire to a writing group, therapy, a support group, and something social; almost every day I try to go to a local café and write.

It's extremely ironic that I would have developed such a regular system. When I was hospitalized for depression years ago, the first therapy session every morning was called "Scheduling." You were handed a sheet of blank graph paper, and told to fill in what you had planned for that day, the next day, the week. I hated it with a passion, as did many of my fellow patients, and we used to sneak out to the cafeteria for coffee and bagels until that session was over. To me, structure meant the death of serendipity. It was a ball and chain, a lock with no key, and I felt imprisoned enough already by my illness and my surroundings.

But "structure is essential to mental health" was the message I kept hearing, and I guess I heard it often enough from doctors I respected that I finally, grudgingly, succumbed to the notion. True, every so often I'll rebel against the regimentation of my daily routine. Do I have to get up? Do I have to go out? But once the stupid strep throat deprived me of my structure, I absolutely craved it. I realized what a lost and aimless wanderer I am without my well-worn path.

When you're sick, there's nothing to do but lie still and ponder. So I pondered away, not a very smart thing to do when you're feverish. Only five days, and I could already hear the mood goblins whispering—so seductive, so alluring. Come back to us, they beckoned; you know the way. And they were right: I knew it all too well. It's so easy to stumble into that black crevasse when I'm bored and have nothing better to do. Time has no meaning there. An hour is endless. There is nothing to stop me from falling forever.

Alarmed, I took out a blank piece of paper, sketched a rough graph of hours and activities, and taped it up on my refrigerator. Seven a.m.: get up, have coffee, check emails, watch the news. Eight a.m.: make breakfast, return emails. Nine a.m.: call Mom, pay bills. And so forth. I could almost hear the snickers of my former compatriots at the hospital.

"You're scheduling!" they'd say.

"Damn right, and you should, too," I'd reply. "Who are we, of all people, to invite chaos into our lives?"

An unplanned life may sound rebellious and free-spirited, and I suppose for some it is. But I need a map with clearly marked boundaries that don't fall off the edges into "Here Be Dragons" land. I need to see where I'm going, and how I'll get there. Of course, I know I don't have to adhere to the schedule. If I want, I can tear it into tiny bits and watch reruns of "Downton Abbey" until I'm thoroughly stupefied. But when the mood goblins come to call and I have to fight them, it's comforting to know that I'm not faced with forever—that I can take eternity one hour at a time. It's a much fairer fight that way.

— — —

VIGILANCE: AM I TOO, TOO WONDERFUL?

I woke up feeling rather strange, and couldn't quite put my finger on it. Was I sick? No, I felt fine. Was something bad supposed to happen that day? Not that I could remember. I brushed my teeth, took a shower, got dressed. Gradually, I forgot to worry. In fact, worry was the very last thing on my mind.

I felt—are you ready for it?—content.

I don't traffic all that much in simple contentment, so it's not a trusted feeling. Don't get me wrong: It's not that I haven't had my fair share of joy. Great joy, in fact. Exuberance, ecstasy, exaltation. Bipolar disorder has taught me everything there is to know about the extremes of elation. When I'm manic, there's nothing unusual at all about skyrocketing high above the clouds, burning through the stratosphere. I see beauty everywhere I look—too much beauty sometimes. I drink it in until I drown.

But this wasn't ecstasy. This was a plain old Tuesday morning. Colors didn't snap and glow, they were just ordinary colors: red, blue, green. My coffee didn't taste like ambrosia, my English muffin was slightly burnt. But still, I felt a marvelous sense of satisfaction with my breakfast: it was perfect, and I was complete.

I didn't know what to do about this, if indeed something had to be done. If it were hypomania, that would be wonderful. But was it a precursor to mania? If so, I wanted no part of it. Flying too perilously close to the sun may be fine—in fact, it can be spectacular—but it always lands me in trouble. And like Icarus, I have the singed wings to prove it: reckless romances, ruined friendships, financial mayhem, even incarceration. So yes, the moment felt lovely—but was it just a moment, or the beginning of something more? In short, was it okay to let down my guard and enjoy my English muffin?

I know all this rumination may sound absurd, but acute self-awareness is one of the prices you have to pay if you want to function with bipolar disorder. You constantly have to check in with yourself: What is my emotional temperature now? Am I running too hot or too cold? Is there an objectively verifiable reason for the way I feel, or is it my chemistry running amok? Nothing, not even joy, comes to me without a cost. Every smile has a price tag attached.

I once tried to explain this to a new boyfriend who was chiding me for, as he put it, "actively resisting pleasure." I told him I was concerned that I was feeling so marvelous because I didn't know why that should be the case.

"Sounds like a champagne problem to me," he said. "Just go with the flow, like I do." (Yes, he spoke like a '70s greeting card and no, we didn't last long.)

"But what if you can't stop laughing, for no good reason?" I persisted. "It doesn't disturb you in the least that you don't know why?"

"I don't care what the cause is," he said, drawing me closer. "I just enjoy the effect."

How I envied his careless insouciance. For me, happiness always needs a hook, a place to hang my emotions on—and I was sure he wasn't it.

So on that plain old Tuesday morning, I looked around me: same stack of laundry on the chair, still not folded; same pile of bills on the table, still unpaid. I glanced out the window: It wasn't a particularly nice day. In fact, it looked rather gloomy, dark gray nimbus clouds threatening rain. And yet, and yet—I couldn't help it. I felt all sunny inside. I buttered my muffin and savored each bite. Then I emailed my therapist: "Feeling awfully good today."

"Careful," he replied.

THE HAPPINESS HUSTLE

Sometimes I feel like life is run by a snooty maître d'. The joy section seems strictly reserved for other people—people who don't have to struggle with their sanity every day. Lucky people. But do they make their own luck, and thus their own joy? It's a question I wrestle with every day: do I work hard enough at being happy?

I have a dear friend, Arnold, who's eighty-six years old and keeps getting battered by cancer. In spite of his hardships, he has the joie de vivre of a child. His grin reaches from ear to ear, it comes sparkling out of his eyes. He cultivates culture like no one I've ever met before: always at this or that premiere, the hottest plays, the coolest restaurants. He's like a burst of jazz that revs you up, that you can't help tapping your feet to. For me, he is quintessential joy.

A few summers ago, Arnold asked me to join him and some of his friends at the Hollywood Bowl (where he has a center box, naturally), to hear the celebrated pianist Lang Lang play with the L.A. Philharmonic, under the direction of the great Gustavo Dudamel. Despite the glittering program, I hesitated before saying yes. I was fighting a severe depression at the time, so bad I had to write down reasons to live. I wasn't sure I could commit to tomorrow, let alone an excursion a whole week away.

Arnold knew I was depressed, and he knew the depth of my depressions. He didn't try to argue me out of my feelings, but he urged me to go with him anyway. "You're a fighter," he said, a huge compliment coming from him. "And besides," he added with a sneaky smile, "it might be material." He understood me all too well—writers can't resist a possible story. With misgivings, I agreed to go.

But when the day of the performance came, my funk was worse than ever. It didn't occur to me that I might feel better if I got out for an evening: that's not how I think in depression. It always feels dangerous to raise my hopes because when they're dashed, I fall even lower than before. It's much safer not to hope at all. At least, that's what I told myself as I sat down at my computer, composing my regrets. I tried out various excuses and lies, but none of them sounded convincing and all of them sounded ungrateful. I finally got so frustrated I just said to hell with it, and threw on some clothes.

Three hot, sweaty, honking hours later I arrived at the Bowl and found the box. Arnold greeted me with a great big hug that I wanted to feel but couldn't. I dutifully smiled my way through introductions and conversation. Although I was hardly in a picnic mood, I filled my plate, chewed and swallowed appropriately. In short, I performed on my own little stage. It's incredibly hard to withstand the beauty of the Bowl—the huge trees framing the Art Deco clamshell, the cobalt twilight, the star-pocked sky—but I tried. I did my best to uphold my stalwart code of depression.

Then the orchestra played "The Star-Spangled Banner," and fifteen thousand people stood up to sing along. As if on cue, a breeze lifted the flag and it waved in allegiance with the music. My eyes began to sting—I blamed the breeze—but before I knew it a tear had rolled down my cheek. A chunk of the ice that was my soul was slowly beginning to thaw.

Lang Lang came out and made love to the piano, while Dudamel seduced the orchestra. It was all very erotic: the light wind on my sweaty neck, the clustered nearness of so many strangers, Tchaikovsky stroking my senses. I tried to resist being touched, being moved—but then I saw out of the corner of my eye that Arnold was so rapt in the music, he was waving his arms like Dudamel, leading us on. The sight was too charming: I couldn't help but smile.

It's scary to let down my defenses when it feels like they're all that's holding me together. But I forced myself to surrender, and let it all flood me: the glorious music and the treasured friendship and the magnificence of the setting. I worked hard at being happy, like Arnold does, and the rewards came tumbling in. I completely forgot that I was depressed, and didn't remember until I got home. But by then it was too late to do anything about it, so I washed my face, conducted a bit of Tchaikovsky in the mirror, and slept until morning.

— — —

SECTION VI

Maintenance

MEDICATIONS

"Canst thou not minister to a mind diseased,
pluck from the memory a rooted sorrow, raze
out the written troubles of the brain . . . ?"
—William Shakespeare (1564–1616),
Macbeth, act 5, scene 3

Antidepressants are the second-most commonly prescribed drugs in the United States, just after cholesterol-lowering drugs. According to the American Psychological Association, most antidepressants are prescribed by primary care doctors "who may have limited training in treating mental health disorders." In the United States, almost four out of five prescriptions for psychiatric drugs are written by physicians who aren't psychiatrists.

And yet, experts believe that psychotropic drugs are both overprescribed *and* underprescribed. Many adults who could greatly benefit from the drugs—those with psychotic disorders, for example, or major depression—do not receive treatment. Stigma ("pill shaming"), financial constraints, a lack of insight into their illness, side effects, and other concerns prevent them from seeking or obtaining help. At the same time, many people with mild or situational depression are prescribed antidepressants even though other treatment modalities, like cognitive behavioral therapy, have proven more effective (https://www.apa.org/monitor/2012/06/prescribing).

Despite the controversy, there is no question that medication plays an essential role in controlling mental illness. As the Mayo Clinic observed, while psychiatric drugs don't provide a cure, they can significantly improve symptoms. They can also help make other treatments, such as psychotherapy, more effective by giving the patient the stability needed to address their problems (https://www.mayoclinic.org/diseases-conditions/mental-illness/diagnosis-treatment/drc-20374974).

Medication compliance isn't easy—it's rather heroic, when you consider how difficult it can be. But it's critical for those of us who need these drugs to live productive, healthy lives. Pill shaming doesn't occur with insulin; there is no reason it should occur with medications used to treat a brain dysfunction.

— — —

MIXOLOGY: THE
MEDICATION COCKTAIL

At one of my recent speaking engagements, an angry young woman brought up the subject of medication compliance. "Why don't people just stay on their meds?" she asked me. "It seems like every time something really bad happens, you hear that the person went off their meds. It's become such a cliché."

There were murmurs of assent in the crowd. Another woman spoke up. "All of you"—all of who, I wondered—"keep telling me that mental illness needs to be treated just like physical illness. Fine, then people should take their medication, just as if they were really sick."

That "really sick" got under my skin, but I understood the woman's frustration. Medication compliance is a hotly emotional topic, and I rant about it, too. It makes me furious when people get into trouble because they've stopped taking their prescribed medication. It tars me with the same stigmatic brush—I must be violent, or dangerous, or a ticking time bomb—even though I steadfastly take my pills every day.

But, and how bipolar is this, I can see both sides of the argument.

Taking meds is really hard. In fact, I doubt most people realize how difficult it is to coordinate all the drugs that are necessary to keep a person with bipolar disorder stable. Many of us—perhaps most—must take a "medication cocktail:" drugs to avoid mood swings; drugs to counteract the side effects of those drugs; drugs to ameliorate the side effects of the side effects drugs, etc., etc. I mean, come on. I have a J.D. and it takes all my mental acuity just to figure it out: which meds need to be refilled when; which should be taken in the morning and which at night; which must be taken with food or on an empty stomach; and annoying little details like whether grapefruit juice is safe. It's mind-boggling, and you need an advanced mixology degree to prepare the perfect cocktail—which is only arrived at by months, sometimes years, of trial and error and constant, ongoing tweaking.

So why do it? People often ask me this (medical doctors, especially): You seem stable enough. Why do you take all these drugs? As if it's a whim, or a joyride, or something that I choose to do because it makes me high. The truth is, without the drugs I'm a mess. Or as my psychiatrist once put it bluntly: "a menace to society." That was back when I was still drinking and didn't take the myriad of warnings on the medication labels seriously. Back when I considered the "Don't mix with alcohol" proscription to be a suggestion, not a mandate.

Doctors don't tell you the secret life of meds when they rip off that scrip and send you toddling off to the pharmacy. Pharmacists don't, either. It's up to you to read the Patient Information Leaflet that sometimes comes with the pills, sometimes not. It's written in teeny-tiny, frequently unintelligible clinical-ese, with a list of potential side effects that quite often includes cancer and death. It takes blind faith in your doctor and the health care system to swallow that innocent-looking capsule and pray that your nose doesn't fall off.

In the end, faith and hope are the key ingredients in any medication cocktail. Faith in your doctors and hope that this last little pill will finally, please God, take the pain away and make you feel normal—or at least like everyone else. If you have bipolar disorder and you believe in Western medicine, you are conscripted into the religion of psychopharmacology, whether you want to believe in it or not.

But hey, I know I'm lucky to be able to afford treatment at all, although it's obscenely expensive. I'm lucky to have found drugs that

work for me, much of the time. So many people never experience relief, and so many refuse to avail themselves of the opportunity. Perhaps, like me, they don't like to feel dependent on anything other
than their self-control. But I've seen the results of my self-control,
and I'm far better off taking drugs. Hence my medication compliance: it's not because I possess better morals, it's just that I have
sufficient evidence of who I was before.

THERE BUT FOR THE
GRACE OF MEDS . . .

I was not happy. I was waiting in line at the pharmacy to pick up a prescription; it was one of my more expensive medications, and I didn't look forward to forking over hundreds of hard-earned dollars. As I waited, I wondered: *Why was I taking this drug, anyway?* It's an atypical antipsychotic, and I've never been psychotic. Maybe that's where the atypical comes in. Who knows? Nobody really understands the mechanisms of these psychotropic medications because nobody really knows what causes bipolar disorder in the first place. It's a frantic rub on a genie's lamp.

But I waited in line, and I got out my credit card because that's what you do when you're medication-compliant: you comply.

The outside door opened, or rather the door was flung open by a middle-aged woman. She was crying, and in a voice loud enough to reach every corner of the pharmacy, she yelled, "I'm not going to f***king jail!" This was followed by a string of curses, which were so profane I'm not even going to try to reproduce them here. I took a quick look at her and backed away, as did the other two people in line with me.

Her clothing was disheveled, her face deeply weathered, and a powerful stench of sweat and urine enveloped her. She didn't look at me or at anyone, for that matter. She just continued to curse in a voice so harsh and guttural it actually hurt my ears. I wanted to leave but she was blocking the exit.

"Call my goddamn doctor!" she shouted. "Do it! Call him! I'm not going to f***king jail!"

I felt dizzy, not because of the smell or my fear, but because I was suddenly plunged deep into déjà vu. It was maybe fifteen years ago, and I was walking along in a shopping mall. Well, "walking" may not be the right word. I was stumbling. Listing. Aspiring to step in a straight line, and failing. I was taking a new drug called a monoamine oxidase inhibitor, or MAOI for short. It was a last-ditch medication for treatment-resistant depression, and if I hadn't been so desperate I never would have taken it.

The side effects were truly debilitating: if you ate pizza or soy sauce or any other food containing a substance called tyramine, you could suffer a fatal stroke. Same if you took it with other antidepressants, or allergy medications. Or alcohol. Niggling little issues like that. But what really concerned me were the unpredictable and severe spells of dizziness I kept experiencing. I was okay so long as I was sitting down, but once I was standing or walking I never knew if I'd find myself fainting in a stranger's arms. There was nothing romantic about these swoons. More often than not, I fell and hit my head or incurred a nasty bruise on my increasingly black-and-blue body.

That particular afternoon I was feeling my usual woozy—so much so that I'd actually taken a cab to the mall, an expensive precaution but I didn't want to risk driving. I took a few shaky steps, and a blinding whiteness engulfed me. I heard a loud buzzing, as if I were suddenly swarmed by bees, but before I could wave them off my knees buckled and I fell to the ground. A sharp searing pain stung my cheekbone. After that, I heard nothing until I was shaken awake by a strange man in a familiar uniform: a cop. Not a mall cop, either. A bona fide pistol-toting, stern-faced policeman.

"What's your name?" he asked. I shook my head free of its fog and told him.

"Let me see some I.D." My hands were shaking—cops make me nervous—but I rummaged through my purse and produced my driver's license.

"But I didn't drive here," I said. "I took a cab because—"

"Ms. Cheney, have you been drinking today?"

I vehemently shook my head no.

"Because you appear intoxicated to me."

"I'm not intoxicated; I just got dizzy, is all." I stood up and damn it, got dizzy again. I clutched the cop's arm for support, and sat back down on the curb.

"Something's not right here," he said. "I'm taking you to the station."

"No, look, it's just this new medication I'm on. I'm fine as long as I'm sitting down, but—"

"The city has strict rules against public intoxication," he said.

"But I'm not intoxicated," I insisted. "It's perfectly legal medication. Here, you can call my doctor and he'll tell you." I fished out my psychiatrist's card from my purse. I carried it everywhere, no matter the occasion, because I felt like he was my proof of sanity and I never knew when I might need that.

"No, I'd better take you in," he said. "For your safety as well as the public's."

That did it. What did he think I was going to do, go on a wobbly-kneed robbing spree? I thrust the card in his hand and heard my voice go shrill, but I couldn't help it. "I'm not going to jail!" I said. "Call my goddamn doctor!"

I was so upset, I started to cry. The cop must have been one of that breed of men who can't bear to see a woman's tears because he paged my doctor, who called him back immediately and confirmed that I was merely experiencing transient side effects from a prescribed medication. I suppose he reassured him that I wasn't a menace to myself or others because the cop finally let me go.

"You know," he said as a parting shot, "just because it's legal doesn't make it okay. You can still be intoxicated even if it's prescribed."

I was too eager to be rid of him to acknowledge the importance of his warning. All I wanted was to get the hell away from there, back to the safety of my own home. I was so rattled I didn't even try to get up. I just sat on the curb and waited for the cab to deliver me from danger.

Fifteen years later, as the homeless woman in my pharmacy grew increasingly agitated, my past echoed as loudly as her screams. "I'm not going to jail! Call my goddam doctor!" was not a cry you heard from every person on the street. We were clearly sisters under the skin, separated only by some inexplicable flick of destiny.

I had been gifted with resources the homeless woman had plainly been denied. My middle-class appearance must have given me a credibility that she unfortunately lacked—people wanted to help me. Plus my illness responded to medication; not always smoothly, but in the end. Perhaps I had a spark of conscience or fear that the woman didn't possess, that kept me med-compliant. But who's to say what her story was?

Someone must have called the police because two cops arrived to take the woman away. Her tears had no apparent impact on them because they were none too gentle as they escorted her out. The pharmacist shook his head as he gave me my pills. "We see her a lot," he said. "You'd think someone would get her some help." I looked at my bottle of atypical antipsychotics, and I looked at the police car just pulling away from the curb. And no, I didn't rush out to save the day. I didn't try to fix fate. But I closed my eyes and said a prayer for her; then I blessed each and every one of the little pink pills I held in my hand.

CHOOSE YOUR POISON

I once was referred to a mental health support group located in a spotless, shiny wing of a spanking new hospital. It was full of articulate, pleasant people, and I felt like I might have found a home. Until I started to share my story, and the leader stopped me.

"We don't talk about medications in here," he said.

"You're kidding."

"It's our policy. We don't want to be seen as giving medical advice."

Well, I thought that was about the stupidest rule I'd ever heard, so I walked out. I've since discovered that many other organizations (many AA chapters, for example) don't discuss psychiatric medications for various reasons. Again, beyond absurd to me. I talk a lot about medications because I take a lot of them, and they're a big part of my life.

In fact, along with really good therapy, meds are the cornerstone of my recovery. I wouldn't be here without them. Which doesn't mean I idealize them, by any means. I probably complain more about my meds than I do about any other subject. But it's my right—I suffer through the damn things.

Like the other night: completely out of the blue, my body decided to revolt. It wouldn't obey my stern command to lie quietly and fall asleep. Instead, I started twitching all over. My knees jerked, my back spasmed, my muscles wouldn't stop fidgeting. I kept trying to find a comfortable position, but the minute I thought I'd found one, some part of me complained. So I got up, stretched, and walked around. The discomfort let up for a second, then returned. I had to keep moving in search of relief.

You know that special agony when you're strapped into a tiny airplane seat, miles above an endless ocean, and all you want to do is move? That's how it felt—like I was on a fourteen-hour flight somewhere, consigned to the purgatory of coach, trying hard not to panic. Except there was no airplane. I was trapped inside my own body.

This lasted all night, and when it showed no signs of dissipating, I left an urgent message for my doctor at daybreak. I knew it had to be my drugs. Whenever something truly bizarre goes wrong with my body, it's always the drugs. I specialize in rare side effects, it seems—like odd rashes and acute photosensitivity and eyelash loss. I'm also not a stranger to the garden variety problems: fatigue, weight gain, acne, tremors, insomnia, blurred vision . . . You name it, I've had it.

But I persist because my mind needs the leash. Sometimes, when my mood is under adequate control, I believe the medication is magic—until it misbehaves and reveals itself for what it truly is: black magic, as much a product of superstition as science. By the time my doctor called me back, I'd worked myself up into a tizzy and had difficulty understanding what he was trying to tell me.

"It sounds like akathisia," he said.

"Aka what?"

"Akathisia. It's a painful, sometimes excruciating inner restlessness, usually caused by the atypical antipsychotics. I can give you something now for the symptoms, but we may have to cut down your dose of those drugs or wean you off them altogether."

That frightened me more than the pain itself. Atypical antipsychotics—the latest generation of psychotropic drugs—are the main ingredient of my medication cocktail. They've made all the difference in the world to my recovery, and I can't imagine my life without them. I told my doctor just that.

"Sometimes you have to make a choice," he said, but what I heard was "You can have your mental health or your physical health. But not both."

Suddenly I felt furious and had to hang up the phone before my rage spewed out all over my doctor. Of course I knew it wasn't his fault (although that didn't stop me from being irrationally angry with him). But whose fault was it? God's? Fate's? What horrible act had I ever committed to be placed in such an untenable position? It wasn't fair, and unfairness is a hot-button issue with me. The more I contemplate the injustice of the universe, the more depression seeps into my psyche and drowns out all remnants of reason.

I decided, ultimately, to stay on the drugs. I knew I would. Physical discomfort may be extremely hard to take, but for me, mental torment is unendurable. And it's dangerous, even deadly, for someone with my history of suicidality. Worst of all, it feels like it's going to last forever—the body at least has its boundaries, but psychic suffering knows no limits. So in the end I chose to protect my mind. But in truth, I wondered: *did I really have a choice?* Mind vs. body: which wins?

SIDE BY SIDE BY SIDE EFFECT

"Oh no, not that!"

"Dear God, make it stop!"

"Somebody call 911!"

Stick around my house long enough in the middle of the night, and you'll be sure to hear me shrieking something along these lines. I wake up in a sweat, shivering and frantic. It takes me a while to remember where I am—that the vampire bats aren't real, the coffin's not mine, the earthquake is all inside my head. It's not my hormones raging, it's my dreams. They're so vivid and terrifying my subconscious can't cope.

I've repeatedly complained to my psychopharmacologist about this. His explanation is that several of my bipolar medications can cause extremely vivid dreaming. "But of course the content of your dreams is up to you," he said. Meaning, I suppose, that if I were saner I could be enjoying the fruits of my drugs and having dreams of wild sex and winning the lottery.

I've experimented with all sorts of ways to reinvent myself as a dreamer. I've tried acupuncture, hypnosis, visualization techniques. I've meditated before falling asleep. I've abstained from spicy foods and alcohol and coffee. I've exercised, not exercised, I've tried it all—all except giving up the pharmaceutical agents that are vivifying my dreams. It's ironic: they keep me sane during half of my life, the part where I'm awake; but they make me quake with terror during the other, more defenseless half.

Does there always have to be a trade-off for sanity?

It's a question I've grappled with most of my adult life, since most of it has been spent taking psychotropic drugs. I can only begin to list the side effects I've had to endure: a forty-pound weight gain from one medication; dangerous fainting fits from another; nausea so intense I was sure I was pregnant; and then the general dopiness, fuzziness, and zombiedom I've come to expect as a matter of course.

My best horrible side effect was when I inexplicably started lactating one day while I was arguing a motion in court (and no, I wasn't pregnant). Milk just started pooling out of my breasts, obvious to anyone who dared to look. The judge took pity on me and asked if I needed a recess. That gave me some much-needed time to look up a case opposing counsel had just cited, which ultimately helped our side prevail. Had it not been for my mental illness, the malfunctioning medication that shot up my prolactin levels, and my resultant leaky breasts, I doubt we ever would have won. Justice, that day at least, was served.

But most of the time, I'm just plain cantankerous about the compromises I have to make. When I travel, it's absurd how much fuss and bother I have to take over my myriad of pills. A few years ago when I went to Dubai to speak about my mental illness—at a psychiatric convention, no less—I was required by the laws of the United Arab Emirates to keep all my psychotropic medications in their original containers; get sworn affidavits from my prescribing doctors; have those affidavits notarized; then get them officially certified by the California Secretary of State. In the end, I had to obtain special permission from the consulate in Dubai to bring my drugs into their country. I try my best to see the dark humor in things, but that episode still makes me fume.

But am I angry and upset enough to stop taking the pills? Not yet. Although I know a lot of people have been helped by alternative remedies, and I definitely believe they have their place in recovery, for me they only last as long as the placebo effect. But when the drugs work, they really work. They keep me alive and relatively balanced and safe. Staying compliant on my meds is a big sacrifice sometimes, but it's one that I'm willing to make and keep on making because right now, drugs feel like my last, best hope. It's the Dark Ages, I grant you—even in ultra-civilized Dubai—but for me they're a glimmer of light.

MIND CANDY: THE EPIDEMIC OF OVERPRESCRIBING

A friend of mine recently told me that he had decided to go off his antidepressant because he felt "too mellow." I stared at him in disbelief. My life with mental illness has been many things—tumultuous, raucous, ecstatic, chaotic—but I would never in a million years describe it as mellow. Mellow was something to aspire to, a far-off goal like nirvana and serenity. How could anyone ever have too much serenity?

"I don't seem to worry as much when I get up in the morning," my friend continued. "It makes it hard to get stuff done." Again, my open-mouthed stare. A troublesome lack of worry sounded frankly absurd to me, and I found it hard not to laugh.

I knew that my friend was not chronically depressed. He didn't have bipolar disorder or social phobia or panic attacks, or any other psychiatric diagnosis that I could put my finger on. What he had was a spate of nasty luck—a series of stressful experiences that had made his life harder than normal and dampened his usual high spirits. He told his primary care doctor about this, and she had whipped out her prescription pad and prescribed the antidepressant. No recommendation or referral to talk therapy, or cognitive behavioral therapy, or even a local support group. Just sleight-of-hand psychiatry—a little bit of magic to balance on the tip of the tongue. A subtle dose of mellow.

I can hear the anger bubbling up behind my words, but I can't help it. It upsets me when psychotropic medications are casually prescribed for situational depression (as opposed to major depression or bipolar disorder). Antidepressants are supposed to address a chemical imbalance in the brain, not just appease a patient who's having a bad month or two. In my opinion, my friend could have benefited immensely from a short round of therapy. And who knows? He might have learned coping skills that would not only help him through his current situation, but serve him in good stead for the rest of his life.

Overprescribing psychiatric meds doesn't just hurt the patient who lacks a viable diagnosis. It makes it worse for the rest of us who really, truly need these drugs to function. Skyrocketing demand naturally drives up the cost, which is already shockingly prohibitive. (Just one—one—of my medications is over $5,000 per month without insurance. And that's no typo.) The drug companies can blithely charge what they like, knowing that every day patients are going to walk into the doctor's office seeking that latest miracle pill they saw on TV, the one that made the sad girl smile.

My friend, like so many other people these days, doesn't have an ongoing relationship with his doctor. He sees her intermittently— there's no real oversight or follow-up. So when I asked him what his doctor had said about how to go off his antidepressant, he looked at me blankly. "I'm just going to stop taking it," he said, at which point I had to get up and walk around the room to release the steam building up between my ears. It's essential to carefully titrate down with an antidepressant, or you risk severe withdrawal. I've been through it, and it's hell. My friend didn't know this because his doctor hadn't told him.

I explained about the need to go off the drug slowly. My friend wasn't convinced, or maybe he was just too mellow to appreciate the seriousness of the situation. "You're making way too big a deal out of this," he said. That's exactly the problem, and that's why I'm so bothered. Drugs *are* a big deal, they're a very big deal, and it's time that we all recognize this—doctors and patients alike. Antidepressants aren't mind candy.

What bothers me most about overprescribing is that it cheapens the experience. Taking psychiatric medication ought to be a solemn thing. Those side effects spelled out in the *Physicians' Desk Reference* and splattered all over Google aren't there simply for shock value. You shouldn't be ready to pop a pill just because your wife's cousin did, or you heard an enticing thirty-second sound bite. The decision to take these meds should be entered into wisely and with reverence: because believe me, it's a sober contract.

BLISS OR LITHIUM?

This past spring, the urge to feel splendid disturbed my sleep: the desire to travel, to see fresh sights, to live a vivid new life without any constraints. I blamed it on the jacaranda trees. Whenever the jacarandas burst into bloom, I feel like I should be blooming, too. Which would be fine, except for one thing: when you have bipolar disorder, full bloom often means full-blown mania, and not even for the siren call of spring was I willing to take that path.

Still, I eyed my lithium warily each night. What would happen if I only took half the dose? The idea was enticing, although I knew that lithium was my friend. But some friends are, frankly, a drag. Lithium helps me stay sane, but it also tamps me down. My creativity suffers, exuberance flees, and I experience a certain degree of cognitive dulling—not unbearable, but by no means pleasant, either. And pleasure was all I was after.

Joy! The whole world seemed steeped in it, from the crabgrass run riot in my neighbor's yard, to the Easter lilies that sprang up from nowhere on my hill, to the songbirds that trilled all the way through dusk. I noticed these things but I didn't inhabit them, not the way I would if I were manic. *Perhaps if my blood weren't so diluted by lithium*, I thought, *it would sing in sympathy with the birds*. My heart would open with the lilies. I'd stare at a solitary stalk of crabgrass until I knew the oneness of many things.

How I longed for my old intensity, even though it wasn't always limited to pleasure. Pain is more difficult to remember, but I knew that it was out there, too, watching me with eager eyes. Lithium may be a barrier to joy, but the numbness does help keep desperation at bay. The trade-off was worth it, or so I kept on telling myself as I stared at the oblong pink capsules in my hand. "It's worth it," I whispered furiously each night, before reluctantly taking the pills.

And yet, I became intensely envious whenever a young woman in my writing group described her latest romantic adventures. She was in ecstasy, she was in agony, she was so tormented by her flood of feelings that she wept every single time she read. I wondered if my writing would take such flights if I weren't so tethered to sanity. What images would enchant my imagination, what words would flutter off my tongue . . . And far more interesting: what would my own love life be like, if I dared to set it free?

They're so tiny, those pale pink capsules. No bigger than my fingernail. And yet how heavily they weighed in my hand. Was it really worth it, after all?

I was debating this again one night when my phone rang. It was my best friend, distraught and sobbing. I gradually pieced her story together: Her daughter had attempted suicide and had just been admitted to a psych ward. What should she do? I gave her what comfort I could, but when I hung up the phone I felt a surge of relief. Thank God, this time it wasn't me. It wasn't my mother having to make those anguished phone calls late at night. Please, can you help me? Please, can you help her? I was here, safe at home, pills in hand. That's when I realized that true joy isn't a flood of bliss. It is, quite simply, a lack of drama. Gratefully, I swallowed my lithium, yet another night.

In a strange stroke of serendipity, the next day I stumbled across a quote from Epicurus (341–270 BC): "Pleasure is the absence of pain in the body and of trouble in the soul." The fact that this was ancient wisdom made me feel even more secure in my epiphany. Pleasure may be heightened intensity for some, but for me real pleasure lies in absence: the absence of too much emotion, too much awareness, too much sensation. Too much tumult, even if the tumult sometimes feels like delight.

THERAPY

"Education never ends, Watson. It is a series
of lessons, with the greatest for the last."
—Arthur Conan Doyle (1859–1930), *His Last Bow*

— — —

It's generally accepted that the most effective treatment for mental illness across the spectrum is a mix of some form of therapy and medication. This is particularly true for major depression. In a large study reported in the *New England Journal of Medicine,* chronically depressed adults given both medication and cognitive behavioral therapy had vastly improved results: "The combination of the two was whoppingly more effective than either one alone," said one of the researchers. "People suffering from [mental illness] often have longstanding interpersonal difficulties, and the virtue of combined treatment in this case may be that it simultaneously targets both symptoms and social functioning."

Simply put, therapy sometimes reaches places where medication can't. As the chief of staff at the Menninger Clinic observed, "Mental illnesses are complicated. Medications can do part of the job, but the rest must be done by a careful part-nership between [therapist] and patient, a thoughtfully crafted treatment plan that includes psychotherapy and/or high-quality psychosocial interventions. It's respect, compassion, genuine interest, and professional expertise that [therapists] must bring to the patient, to form a therapeutic relationship."

Medications alone can't deliver that all-important personal touch. Critical as they are to a successful treatment plan, their benefits may end when you stop taking them. The benefits of therapy, however, endure. That makes it a good investment, ac-cording to *Forbes* magazine: "The positive gains continue and grow over time, as some of the work gets further consolidated after therapy stops."

For those who prefer hard science over warm and fuzzy benefits, consider this: Like medication, therapy can rewire the brain. Imaging studies have shown that psychotherapy can al-ter activity in the medial prefrontal cortex, the anterior cingulate cortex, the hippocampus, and the amygdala—regions involved in executive control, emotion, and fear. It's true, therapy may not be a quick fix or a magic bullet. But a pill can't tell you it cares if you're alive.

— — —

ANNOYING EPIPHANIES

For better or worse, talk therapy is a strip tease. If you're like me, and uncomfortable with your nakedness, it can be unsettling. I want my therapist to like me—a perfectly human desire. But I also want him to see me, warts and scabs and bruises and all, because otherwise why are we wasting our time? It's not perfect skin I came in to fix.

Lately I've been trying to work on my emotional intensity in therapy. Again, it's not something I feel comfortable talking about. I get comments about it all the time, and they invariably feel like criticism. "Can't you just have a normal conversation?" people say. "Do you always have to go so deep?" It embarrasses me, as if I'd opened up a vein in public and didn't realize I was bleeding all over the place. I don't want to become an automaton, just tone things down a bit.

It's a challenge. For as far back as I can remember, I've always felt too much. Even as a little girl, I dramatized the most innocent pastimes. Hide-and-seek terrified me—I was certain that if I hid too well, I'd be lost from sight forever. Tag was even worse. I couldn't stand the suspense of being chased, so I'd just refuse to run. This infuriated my playmates, who tortured me no end. I'd take refuge in the doghouse and cry my heart out until my mother found me in there one day. "Stop it," she said. "You're making the dog neurotic."

What she didn't know, and I didn't either, was that when you're bipolar, life is always bigger than life. Emotions are never just feelings; they're grand-scale productions. Joy isn't joy; it's sheer rapture. Sorrow isn't sorrow; it's utter anguish. Frankly, it's exhausting—and I know it wears out the people around me. I can understand their comments about my intensity. I just thought I hid it better.

It's been hard to make progress on this issue in therapy. Emotions are like cranky children: they don't like being told what to do. "But why can't I be passionate?" I asked my therapist. "Isn't that a good thing? Don't most people want to feel more than they do?"

"Passion is fine, but not when it interferes with your relationships," he said.

"It shouldn't. That's the other person's problem, not mine."

"Then why are you talking about it with me?" he asked.

That stumped me for a moment. "Because—because—you represent the outside world. You can tell me what other people experience. You can tell me what I'm doing wrong."

"There's no right or wrong about it," he said. "It's simply a choice."

I wanted to strangle him (much as I care for him, I sometimes feel that way, although I never act on it). "But that's the thing," I said. "Being intense *isn't* a choice. I'm just hardwired that way."

"Then why are you trying to change?" he asked.

I suddenly felt very, very small and started to tear up. "Because it hurts," I said. "People criticize me for being me, and it hurts."

Now and then my therapist belies his kooky Hawaiian shirts and comes out with something truly insightful. "Pain is inevitable," he said to me. "Suffering is not."

I nodded, trying to look as if I understood, wanting him to feel good about his advice. In truth, I didn't get it. Pain and suffering—weren't they the same thing? That's how we always referred to them in the law: "Plaintiff is entitled to monetary damages for his pain and suffering." I couldn't see the difference. But his words felt important to me somehow, and I kept thinking about them long after I left the office.

Later that night as I was falling asleep, I got it: The essential distinction was time. Pain is abrupt and immediate—it strikes like a rattlesnake, sharp and sudden. But suffering evolves: It's what we choose to do with that pain over time. Do we embrace it, make room for it in our hearts and bodies, allow it to come in and make itself at home? It seems strange that anyone would ever adopt a rattlesnake, but that's what suffering really is: petting the pain that bites you.

I had to ask myself: Despite being bipolar and prone to extreme feelings, did I sometimes overindulge in my emotions? And the answer was unavoidable: hell, yes. I have, after all, written three memoirs about my internal struggles. I attend weekly therapy, two writing groups, and a mental health support group. For years I've mined my misery for raw material—I've examined it from every angle and wooed its every nuance. I've become a bona fide connoisseur of angst.

Although I hated to admit it, I wasn't gaining any further insight into life by being so intense all the time. Was my illness responsible, or had it just become an excuse for a bad habit—and did it even matter? It certainly wasn't helping me, or the people around me. The truth was, I was petting my pain, and I wanted—I needed—to change.

That's the rotten and wonderful thing about therapy. It's supposed to smooth your way through life, but sometimes it starts you on a whole new, and more grueling, journey. I knew I was in for a long, hard road of discovery, but I didn't have the slightest idea how to start. So I did what I've always done when something really scary pursues me: I stopped dead in my tracks and refused to run. Then I reached into my bedside drawer and pulled out my journal.

"For as far back as I can remember, I've always felt too much," I wrote. And so the journey began. Again.

THE RIGHT FIT

In 1998 I checked myself into the UCLA Neuropsychiatric Institute. I was on perilous ground. I had just been arrested for the second of two back-to-back DUIs and was looking at mandatory jail time. My attorneys had immediately thrown me into rehab because they knew it was the best way to show the judge that my remorse for my conduct was sincere. And it was—legal tactics aside, I truly wanted to change. I had finally had enough of suicide attempts and shattered relationships and poisoned dreams and the broken promises at the bottom of a bottle of vodka. I didn't want to be in a mental hospital, but I wasn't ready for real life, either. I was willing to do whatever it took to reclaim my sanity, but I urgently needed help.

And I didn't get it. Not at first, anyway. Those first few "newbie" weeks in the mental hospital were nothing short of terrifying. Doors slammed locked behind me; the windows were barred; the rooms smelled like ammonia, stale coffee, and sour laundry. Patients wearing thick bandages around their wrists wandered the halls, carrying on intense conversations with things that weren't there. People erupted into screams in the middle of therapy sessions, for no apparent reason. One day a man in the common room suddenly stood up and ripped off all his clothes, then poured himself a cup of coffee and sat down as if nothing were amiss. A young woman who must have weighed less than eighty pounds silently pulled out clumps of her hair, leaving angry bald patches behind.

Was I the only one who noticed these things? Sometimes it felt like it, and I began to doubt my senses, and what little reason I could still lay claim to. I was scared, scared, scared every minute of every day—not just of the patients, but of the obvious burnout of many of the doctors and staff. They were dead in their eyes, if not in their hearts. The case worker I had been assigned to barely looked at me as she scribbled in my chart. "Gang history?" she asked me. "Varsity cheerleader," I replied, and she didn't even blink.

A week or so after I got there, during an occupational therapy group (think moccasins and macramé), I was accosted by a middle-aged woman named Sal, who might have been pretty once but had obviously been beaten down by illness and hardship. Her long blond hair was tangled and dirty, her features ravaged by prolonged exposure. "I hear you're a lawyer," Sal said. I nodded, not wanting to interact but afraid to be rude. "You look like a Beverly Hills rich bitch to me."

"I'm here to get help," I said, "just like you." I glanced over at the counselor, who was staring out the window.

"We don't need no rich bitches in here," Sal said. "Why don't you call your sugar daddy to come take you home?"

Some of the other patients took up the chant: "Rich bitch, rich bitch."

The counselor finally glanced over. "Quiet," was all she said. No one paid the slightest attention to her.

Sal stood in front of me and pointed to the door. "Get out, rich bitch," she said. "You obviously don't belong here. What do you know about anything? You've still got all your teeth."

I couldn't answer that. I knew what she meant: What possible claim could I lay to real suffering, with all the blessings I had enjoyed? I didn't deserve help, I deserved to be censured for ruining such a life—a life of comfort and privilege that most of these people would never even catch a glimpse of. I got up and walked to the door. Sal threw a moccasin after me, hitting me in the back of the head.

"Where do you think you're going?" the counselor said to me. "The bell doesn't ring for another ten minutes."

I sat down as close to her as I could get. It was a very long ten minutes. I could feel Sal's eyes, and the eyes of the other patients, burning into my skin. When the bell rang, I bolted to the ladies' room and locked myself into a stall, tucking my legs up on the toilet so nobody could see me. I waited, but no one came in. The bell for the next session rang, and I stayed where I was. Fifteen, thirty minutes went by. *If I could just stay there till dinner time*, I thought, *another half hour or so, I'd be safe.* It was hardly a desirable hiding place—it was damp and smelled nasty—but I was long past caring about such things. It was as close to being invisible as I could get.

I meant to be strong, I meant to be wily, but damn it, I was all alone with my thoughts—something I'd tried very hard to avoid since my second DUI arrest. Unbidden, tears started to flow down my face. What a sorry, sullied mess I'd made of my life. I tried to stanch the tears with strip after strip of the wafer-thin toilet paper, but they just kept on coming. The full impact of my reckless and culpable conduct finally hit me—denial is damn near impossible when you're crouched on a toilet in a mental hospital, hiding out for your life. I gave up trying to cry silently and wailed like the lost and desperate beast I had become.

There was a knock on the bathroom door. I froze.

"Is somebody in there?" a male voice said. "Come on now, I heard you, you might as well come out."

At least it wasn't Sal, I thought; and I had always fared better with men than with women. I clambered down stiffly and opened the door. To my immense relief, it was Roberto, the janitor who always grinned at me in the hallway and called me "Red."

"Hey Red, you know they been looking for you all over the place?" he said. "You got a lot of folks worried."

"It's no use, Roberto," I sobbed. "I'll never make it in here."

"Well frankly, I never really thought you belonged here in the first place," he said. "They got other places you could go, where it's a little more your speed. You just come along with me now, I'm gonna take you to meet Mrs. T." He held out his hand, and I took it.

Mrs. T, it turned out, was high up in the hospital hierarchy; I hadn't met her in the admissions process. She had a thick accent (I later learned her family was from war-torn Bosnia) and china blue eyes that seemed to glow with compassion. I've heard many a doctor fake a soothing voice upon demand, but I've never yet met anyone who could convincingly simulate kindness. She listened to me rave about my situation for what seemed like an hour before she smiled and said, "The answer is simple, my dear. You belong in IOP—our intensive outpatient program."

Outpatient sounded like Paris to me, like the kiss of a faraway breeze. "But they want to punish me for what I've done, and outpatient would give me more freedom," I said. "Judge Rubinsky would never go for that."

"You just leave Aaron to me," she said. I was extremely impressed that she knew his first name and felt comfortable enough to bandy it about. I was practically taught to genuflect before judges.

But sure enough, not long after that the order came down—I was to be transferred to the five-days-a-week outpatient program, pending further direction from the court. My sentencing hearing was three months away. That meant I had three months to get so squeaky clean and sober that I could spark mercy in the soul of a bored and case-hardened autocrat.

I can't say it was easy, even with my move to outpatient status. Although Sal and her gang were locked up six floors above me, there were still plenty of tortured psyches in the day program. But they were recognizably tortured, like I was: not by unknowable demons, but by depression, anxiety, trauma, mania, OCD. Even the psychotic patients were more toned down—still frightening in their otherness, but only intermittently symptomatic. And so many of us, at least two-thirds by my estimate, had a dual diagnosis, meaning we were plagued by alcohol and drug addiction in addition to our mental illness. There was, in short, a lot of common ground.

It was that common ground that began to heal me—not the lectures by the doctors, not the endless medication trials, not the six hours of assorted therapies a day, but the lingua franca of shared suffering. I made friends with people I never would have met on the outside because I would have thought them too strange and different from me, or our paths would simply never have crossed. But I saw myself now in their troubled eyes, and I cried for their pain as well as my own. I rejoiced in their victories, however subtle. Slowly, almost imperceptibly, I started to change. When I shared my story, it was no longer about what "they" were doing to me. It was about how I was hurting myself.

Humility, like healing, doesn't happen all at once. It comes by degrees—a flash of insight here, a brief recognition there. By watching the other patients struggle, I began to realize the extraordinary value of traits I'd always sidelined before: empathy, patience, honesty—not necessarily weapons you'd find in an ambitious litigator's arsenal. Most important of all for my recovery, I learned that mental illness exists on a continuum. It comes in all different shapes and sizes, and treatment has to mirror that. The secret to success is to search for the right fit, then stick with it. I must have gone to thirty different AA meetings before I found one that I could stand, then begin to like, then treasure. It's the same with meds, or therapy. If you just keep looking, you'll feel it when you find it: a safe harbor, a place where you can drop your guard and let body and mind and spirit renew.

To my astonishment, I found that right fit in the outpatient program, as witnessed by the fact that I stayed there three years, which is surely some kind of record. Do I regret that ellipsis from "real" life? No. I went in splintered; I came out as whole as was possible for me. Mental illness still scares me sometimes—but only untreated illness, especially when it's exacerbated by substance abuse. But I'm no longer terrified of being alone with myself.

TRIED AND TRUE

I underwent twelve rounds of ECT (electroconvulsive therapy, commonly known as electroshock) in 1994—or at least that's what my records say. I remember only fits and spurts of that year, and what I do remember is pretty damn scary. But then, it was a scary time. I was at the height of my professional career and the nadir of my personal life, so profoundly depressed I didn't care what they did to my brain so long as they made it work again. Of course, I'd read *One Flew over the Cuckoo's Nest* and seen what horrors ECT had wreaked on Jack Nicholson in the movie. But surely, that was just dramatic license—my doctors wouldn't let me do anything that was truly dangerous, right?

I wonder now how any doctor gets informed consent for a radical treatment from a suicidally depressed patient. It didn't matter to me back then whether I lived or died, I just wanted the never-ending pain to stop. I was willing to believe in anything that offered relief, and oh, the promise of ECT! It was the last resort for severe "treatment-resistant" depression, and it almost always worked, my psychiatrist had told me. Naturally, there were bound to be side effects from having seizures electrically induced in my brain—significant memory loss the most common among many. *But what in my miserable life did I want to remember*, I thought at the time. Forgetting this harsh and brutal existence would be a mercy, not a deficit.

Three separate doctors (as required by my insurance company, which ended up paying for very little because my depression was deemed a pre-existing condition) examined me inside and out and pronounced me a good candidate for ECT. I did my best to convince them of this. Desperate as I was for help, I was a terrified proponent of the procedure, which may sound oxymoronic—although perhaps not for a lawyer who got her start doing criminal appeals, defending rapists' and murderers' rights to a fair trial. I am capable of great cognitive dissonance.

And the ECT worked, to a certain extent. It lifted the depression that had been weighing me down for so long. But in the process I was untethered, hurled into a manic episode that went higher and lasted longer than any I'd known before. I went textbook crazy—spending every last penny I'd ever saved, engaging in reckless, carefree sex with strangers, taking extraordinary risks with my own life and others'. When I finally came down to earth, reality had disappeared and in its place was a new world where I couldn't remember what my middle initial stood for. I had to ask my mother.

ECT has since been improved, or so I've come to believe. Different techniques are now being used that supposedly lessen the risk of memory loss: unilateral vs. bilateral placement of the electrodes, for example, and briefer pulses of electricity. In the support group I facilitated at UCLA up until a few years ago, I witnessed patient after patient undergo the procedure with great success. The ones with the best outcomes were treated more frequently and had regular, ongoing "maintenance" sessions. I'd watch them emerge from hopeless, practically catatonic states to become productive and functioning people again. Sometimes it seemed near-miraculous.

But miracles are magic, and recovery takes hard work. Even when ECT is successful, further treatment is required to sustain the progress. This means, in most cases, a good old-fashioned combination of medication and talk therapy. Of course, there are many alternative therapies as well, and I've had the dubious luxury of trying dozens of them. Here is a sampling of what's worked for me, and what hasn't:

COGNITIVE BEHAVIORAL THERAPY

This is a type of talk therapy in which you identify distorted perceptions and how they impact your emotions and behavior. For

example, black-and-white thinking, in which no shades of sub-
tlety are allowed to exist. Or globalization, in which *everything* is
wrong and *everybody* hates you. There are many such distortions,
which you can find online just by googling "cognitive distortions."
I'm guilty of almost all of them, and it helps tremendously when
I realize it and can reorder my thinking to reflect reality. Having
a therapist trained in this technique to guide you is a bonus, but
you have to do the homework yourself. CBT has been heavily researched, and no other form of psychotherapy has been shown to be
systematically superior.

EMDR

I hesitate to tell you what this stands for because it's so absurdly
technical: eye movement desensitization and reprocessing. Trust
me—the technique itself is a whole lot simpler than the name.
EMDR is essentially a trauma processing technique that helps the
patient confront, and work through, painful memories. When it was
first developed, patients would watch their therapist move his finger
back and forth as they recalled a traumatic event. Both of you felt
pretty silly—until it started to work.

Now there are flashing light boards, or pulsing devices you hold
in each hand, which feel a little more scientific. But the method
doesn't seem to matter: The point is to provide bilateral stimulation.
Some say this darting back-and-forth movement resembles REM
sleep; others say it connects the right and left hemispheres of the
brain. Whatever the mechanism, it's benefited me tremendously,
and I'd love to see it more commonly used.

AA AND OTHER TWELVE-STEP RECOVERY PROGRAMS

The rooms are dingy. People smoke and there's too much hugging.
The canned wisdom can make you gag. All so true, and so beside the
point. Jargon alert: AA works if you work it. You have to find the

right room, the right people, the words that speak directly to you and cut through all the smoke. They're out there, and I have over two decades' worth of sobriety to prove it.

A word of caution, though: I've come across a shocking amount of prejudice in some meetings against taking prescribed medication for mental illness. This runs directly contrary to the founding principles of AA and its progeny, but nonetheless, the ignorance exists and it's dangerous. I suggest downloading a copy of the pamphlet, "The A.A. Member—Medications and Other Drugs," an official A.A. publication that clearly supports the use of psychiatric medication in sobriety (if taken, of course, as prescribed).

WRITING AND NARRATIVE THERAPY

Writing has been a godsend for me. I've been in the same writing group for over fifteen years and have taken as many classes and courses as I can, all with the same ultimate goal: bearing witness. I firmly believe that Socrates was right, that the unexamined life is not worth living. On a more practical level, journaling helps me track my moods so I can fine-tune my medication; research even shows that creative writing may help improve the immune system's functioning. What I know beyond a doubt is that writing has kept me alive—I want to see how the story ends.

MINDFULNESS AND MEDITATION

These are highly in vogue in the medical field right now, and rightly so. One of the most destructive aspects of mental illness is harmful and excessive rumination—about the miseries of the past and the projected woes of the future. Mindfulness encourages you to be in the present, and meditation helps you to achieve that state of awareness. It takes practice, but I know it's a more enlightened way of being so I'm willing to keep working at it, although I have a nagging feeling that it shouldn't be so hard.

ART THERAPY

When I was hospitalized, I balked when I heard that "art therapy" was going to be one of my required sessions. Balked is putting it mildly; I flat out refused to go. I pictured crocheted belts and beaded bracelets and lopsided ashtrays. I seriously doubted whether my insurance would cover such nonsense. And besides, I was a grown-up and a professional—I made deals, not découpage. While I may have been sick, I still had my pride.

But crafts turned out to be only a small, and optional, part of the therapy. The rest of the program was much more varied: role-playing, painting, singing, telling stories, and the like. And to my amazement, the best results I saw in the hospital were not achieved through medication or process groups but through art therapy. Patients who refused to speak up during the other groups somehow found their voices through their unleashed creativity, and let others—including their doctors—know their secret suffering. It was a joy and a wonder to watch.

EXERCISE THERAPY

When you live in Southern California, it's practically a statutory requirement that you try yoga. I have, and it's wonderful—if I'm not really depressed. Exercise of any kind, even walking, is impossible then because of the extreme psychomotor retardation and physical paralysis that overcome me. But that's just me. I know that numerous studies have shown the great efficacy of exercise for moderate depression, and people are always telling me in glowing terms about their endorphin rushes. I envy them, and I kind of wish they'd shut up.

BIOFEEDBACK

This is a noninvasive procedure in which electrodes are attached to your body, and you watch a screen that reflects your brain activity via functional magnetic resonance imaging (fMRI). The goal is to enable patients to voluntarily control the activity of certain regions of the brain. I spent months hooked up to a machine, watching my alpha and beta waves rise and fall. It made me severely anxious, to the point where the doctor—who said he'd never seen this technique fail before—gave up on me and quit.

HYPNOTHERAPY

Once, in a show where members of the audience were hypnotized, I got up on stage and ate a raw onion, which I'd been told was a delicious Fuji apple. I'm highly suggestible. Years later, I tried hypnotherapy for chronic insomnia, without success. But I liked the feeling of relaxation and deep focus I experienced, so I'm not crossing this off my list.

There are many, many other therapies that I haven't yet tried, but would like to: for example, dialectical behavior therapy (DBT), which helps with emotion regulation and is particularly effective with suicidality; and the psychedelics, like ketamine and LSD. I've seen some amazing results from both these treatments, and I'm sure I'll get around to them in time. After all these years of experimenting with my brain, I still believe an answer is out there. I just have to keep reformulating the question.

Therapy of any kind is inherently mysterious, since we don't really know why mental illness occurs in the first place. But one thing is certain: The way a therapy is administered makes a big difference. If it's pitched with enough kindness and confidence, anything can work. The placebo effect is well documented; it's more than just "fake medicine." In clinical trials, people with schizophrenia and depression have exhibited a particularly strong placebo response, and researchers at Harvard Medical School believe they are well on their way to corralling its biochemical basis. It's a thrilling idea—let the mind heal the mind, and Big Pharma, beware.

Ultimately, treatment is a tricky balancing act. There's a lot of good help out there, along with some bad. Take your hope with a good dose of common sense, but do take it.

— — —

SECTION VII

Warranties

ACCEPTANCE

"Be yourself. Everyone else is already taken."
—Oscar Wilde (1854–1900)

— — —

In recovery terms, acceptance of one's mental health situation means not only acceptance of the diagnosis but of the need for treatment, and even associated limitations and consequences. Acceptance of stigma is a thornier question: should one ever accept what is morally and intrinsically wrong?

The National Alliance on Mental Illness promotes "radical acceptance," a term popularized by Marsha Linehan, founder of the dialectical behavior therapy (DBT) technique. This means "completely and totally accepting something from the depths of your soul, with your heart and your mind," she says. If you truly accept your mental health condition, you don't waste valuable energy trying to pretend that it doesn't exist. Rather, you turn your resistant ruminating into forward movement, by taking the necessary steps to care for yourself instead (https://www.nami.org/Blogs/NAMI-Blog/January-2019 /Self-Help-Techniques-for-Coping-with-Mental-Illness).

This doesn't happen overnight. It's a coping skill that requires practice because it doesn't come easily and it doesn't mean that you are then magically immune to the sorrows, fear, and sadness that naturally inhabit all our lives. But the wonderful thing is, you don't have to worsen the situation by adding the pain and struggle of nonacceptance to it. You accept that being human encompasses both good and bad, darkness and light. As J. R. R. Tolkien so poignantly noted, "not all tears are an evil."

— — —

DIAGNOSIS: THE GOOD NEWS?

When you live in L.A., you have to expect that people are going to try to explain bad things by telling you that "Mercury is in retrograde." If you're like me and you don't know what the hell that means, you just nod and say, "Thanks, that makes sense." Like everyone else, I cling to any explanation that might pierce the daily murk. It's bedrock human nature—lost as we are, we'll follow any path to enlightenment.

I think this is one of the reasons I've come to accept my diagnosis of bipolar disorder to the surprising extent that I do. The very idea that my amorphous, inexplicable emotions have clustered together into a syndrome that I can describe in two words excites me and gives me hope. But believe me, I wasn't always like this. For the first half of my life, I knew something was wrong but I refused to investigate the possibilities. The fact that there was a raging monster inside me was obvious, but I didn't want to find out what kind of monster it was. I just wanted it to go away.

Even when I reluctantly started to examine my emotions in psychotherapy, it wasn't an easy task to find the correct diagnosis. It was like looking for the perfect pair of jeans, or worse yet, the perfect bathing suit. I had to face the mirror naked for an uncomfortable period of time and endure an endless amount of trial and error.

Dysthymia was my first diagnosis: a low-grade general misery that was just noxious enough to be recognized (if not reimbursed) by my insurance. I admire the doctor who gave me that wrong diagnosis, and I don't think it was her fault. I hid my howling so well that all she heard was a mournful peep. Eventually, she upgraded me to major depression, which was still the wrong diagnosis but much closer to the core of my condition. By then, I had learned to trust her more and invite her into my mind; so she could see that the monster was much, much bigger than she had originally guessed.

As is the case with so many people who have bipolar disorder, it took years—almost a decade—before I was properly diagnosed. And that only happened by a fluke. I was in the middle of a course of electroshock therapy for an excruciating episode of depression. Without warning, I got zapped into mania. For the first time ever, my doctors saw the amped-up, jazzy side of me that I'd always kept hidden from them. I didn't hide it intentionally. I just felt so good when I was manic that I didn't bother to keep my appointments.

With my new diagnosis came new medications, and to my surprise, some of them actually helped—along with getting sober, which allowed the meds to work without outside interference. Even stranger, I felt less shame about being bipolar than "just" being depressed. Bipolar has a tinge of the exotic to it, like a rare plant that needs special handling. Whereas everybody claims they've been depressed, and I had trouble making people understand the difference between chemical depression and the everyday blues.

My bipolar diagnosis explains so many things about me that used to be a mystery: the wild volatility, the odd combination of ferocity and fragility, the sudden spurts of creativity. It's no wonder that I cling to the clinical label. It lifts me up from denial, to glide on the wings of science. Let Mercury be in retrograde—my own world is so much clearer to me now.

SHADES OF TRUE LIGHT

I've been feeling good lately, which is always hard for me to admit. I've noticed this is true of a lot of people with bipolar disorder: We're afraid we'll jinx the normalcy. Or maybe we're afraid we won't be believed when the bad days strike again. Whatever the reason, I'm scared to say it, but it's true: I feel surprisingly good.

When I'm doing well, I always take advantage of my newfound energy to seek out "a dose of beauty," as my therapist calls it. It's the best nonprescription medicine I know. And the greatest beauty I can imagine comes from Johannes Vermeer, the seventeenth-century Dutch painter and my all-time favorite artist. Most people know him for his *Girl with a Pearl Earring*, but he's so much more than that. He's a rare jewel: exquisite, multifaceted, and extremely hard to find. I once maxed out my last remaining credit card to travel to a Vermeer exhibit at the National Gallery, only to be surrounded by so many other admirers I could barely see a thing. I left in disgust. You have to have moments alone with great beauty, so it can work its way inside.

On a quick jaunt to New York a few months ago, I went on a pilgrimage again. I found him: three Vermeers at the Frick Collection, and another four at the Met. At the Frick, I waited until everyone else had cleared the gallery before I allowed myself to look. I stepped up to *An Officer and a Laughing Girl*, my head bowed as if I were in church. Then slowly, inch by inch, I raised my chin and let the painting in.

There, at last: the light.

Everyone who loves Vermeer remarks, of course, on his use of light—how it falls oh-so-naturally through the ubiquitous windows on the left to flood the scene with warmth. I saw the wondrous light; I sighed in recognition, but this time I also saw something else. For the first time in my life, I saw the shadows. Now of course they had to be there all along, right? Truly depicted light must cast a shadow, and no one is truer to nature than Vermeer. But why had I never seen them before? And why was I seeing them now?

I thought about this all the way back to L.A., and even after that. The answer finally came to me: I simply didn't want there to be shadows before. I wanted to believe there was one place on earth I could go where there was never any gloom, just a splendiferous glow. But perhaps I'm growing strong enough to accept that life demands a balance. How will we recognize rapture if we haven't first felt sorrow? We can't. Pleasure is indebted to pain.

I know this duality in my bones—I live it because I'm bipolar. Which doesn't mean I haven't railed against it for many years. But I feel a tender acceptance growing inside me, and I don't want to disturb it. I'm not wearing blinders: today I may celebrate my strength; tomorrow I may lose myself in my struggle. But when I can't believe in anything else, I can always believe in Vermeer. He's tangible, irrefutable proof that my soul was once calm and still enough to accept true beauty—light and shadow, intermixed. And to my surprise, I welcome those shadows. I think I'm ready for them now.

— — —

HOPE

"You must think that something is happening within
you, and remember that life has not forgotten you;
it holds you in its hand and will not let you fall."
—Rainer Maria Rilke (1875–1926),
Letters to a Young Poet

— — —

A recent Cambridge University study examined "the importance of hope against other factors in the recovery of mental illness." It concluded that "the central tenet in recovery is hope—it is the catalyst for change, and the enabler of the other factors involved in recovery to take charge" (https://www.ncbi.nlm.nih.gov/pubmed/28953841).

Important as it is, hope can be maddeningly elusive. As trauma therapist Jonathan Foiles observes, "Hope can seem like a radical, even foolish, act. In times of despair, it can seem naive or dangerous to think that things may get better." This fundamentally misunderstands the nature of hope, he says. "To be hopeful is to acknowledge that the future remains unwritten and that we have the ability to play a part in its making"

(https://slate.com/technology/2018/06/a-trauma-therapist
-explains-how-to-cope-with-existential-despair.html).

Many of us caught in the web of mental illness doubt our capacity to make the changes in ourselves and the world that seem necessary for personal, and societal, recovery. But giving up hope altogether just doesn't work when you're human. Hope is bred into our bone marrow; it's what keeps our blood pulsing, day after day, no matter what. Instinct knows what we sometimes don't: just keep moving. Hope is an active verb.

But what about when you're paralyzed by depression, or immobilized by anxiety, or rendered inert by suffering? How then do you move? You have to redefine movement—it isn't necessarily physical action. Sometimes it isn't even conscious thought. It's desire, which is always simmering somewhere deep inside us. Desire to change, to have a fuller, richer, more dream-worthy life. As the Cambridge University study found, "Recovery depends on the notion that a patient desires to get better."

So many of us are told to readjust our goals because we're mentally ill, which is fine so long as it doesn't lower our opinions of our intrinsic worth. We deserve more than mere survival. We deserve hope. That hope may be tempered; so is steel.

———

NEW LOVE: HANDLE WITH CARE

"You're so fragile." I used to love hearing that. I thought it made me sound delicate, like an early Renaissance madonna. And very, very costly, like the best bone china or the finest platinum filigree. All the really good pieces in any museum are fragile, I'd proudly tell myself each time the word materialized in a friend's conversation. What I didn't say, because I didn't want to hear it, was that the most fragile pieces are also the ones roped off from the public and labeled DO NOT TOUCH in forbidding capital letters.

I really want to start dating again. After endless bouts of dehumanizing depression, my libido is finally waking up and declaring it's time. But the apparent consensus seems to be that I'm too breakable to venture back into love. "You'll fall apart," my best friend tells me. "Remember the last time you got rejected," my therapist warns. And "Oh my God, not again," my mother says, saying it best.

But the blood is loud in my veins these days, so insistent it muffles these far-off voices of reason. All I want to hear is an earnest whisper in my ear, and I've got the whisperer all picked out. Yes, I want to say to him. Yes and yes. And who knows what might have happened if in the middle of our first kiss, he hadn't pulled back, looked tenderly into my eyes, and said, "Please don't fall in love with me."

That voice was a little harder to ignore. "Excuse me?" I said.

"I don't want to hurt you."

"You're not hurting me," I assured his worried eyes, smiling. "Far from it."

"That's not what I mean," he said, refusing to be distracted by my fingers' light, slow dance on the back of his neck. I sighed, dropped my hands, and resigned myself to listening.

"The last thing in the world I want is for you to get depressed again," he said. "You're just so . . . well, so . . ."

"So what, exactly?"

"Fragile," he whispered into my ear, for all the world as if it were an endearment.

It was brisk that night in Malibu; his balcony directly over-looked the beach. Our kiss—or rather, the feverish tension leading up to it—had made me forget about the cold altogether. But at the sound of that all-too-familiar word, I suddenly started to shiver.

He asked me if I wanted a robe, and I nodded, teeth chattering too hard to speak. "Back in a minute," he said, sliding the glass door shut behind him. I walked over to the edge of the balcony and stared down into the inscrutable black heart of the ocean. It was a calm, serene evening everywhere except inside my head. The full moon reflected off the surface of the water; it winked at me every time a wave rippled across its face. Quicksilver flashes shot through the breakers—little snatches of moonlight, perhaps, or a school of tiny phosphorescent fish. The elemental beauty of the scene quieted me. It was a simple problem, really, almost mathematical in nature: Did I dare to take this risk? If one kiss led to another, and another, and so on up the emotional investment scale, what were the odds of my survival?

I have tremendous fear and respect for suicidal depression. My medications seemed to be working, but nobody really knows why, or how long they can conquer the devil incarnate. A chill went through my bones and my teeth sounded like castanets—all over one little kiss and a handful of damnably ambiguous words. What exactly did he mean by that, anyway: "You're so fragile. Don't fall in love with me . . ."

Was he truly concerned about my safety? Or was he just an arrogant jerk? Or was he maybe, regrettably, right on the money? This last possibility sank in slowly, painfully. "Beware," said the twitching moon in the water. "Beware," said the undertow, sucking in its breath. A line of silver still flashed along the breaking waves, but now it looked like a cruel steel blade, slicing across the ocean's throat. Can I handle love? I asked the night. I heard all my friends' voices reverberating inside my head—and the chorus of "No, no, no" was almost as deafening as the surf.

I was less angry than bewildered by the vote of no confidence ringing in my head. My friends seemed to share an underlying assumption that if I just didn't get involved with a man, time would stand still and I'd keep getting better. But nature doesn't work that way—especially not human nature; especially not when you're bipolar and change is the only certainty you know.

For all its tranquil beauty that night, the ocean had turbulent edges. As sure as the next rising wave would crash, I, too, would fall again—for some reason or other. It might as well be love.

The click of the sliding door startled me back into the present, and again I shivered, this time from anticipation. He stepped out onto the balcony, carrying two thick white terry cloth robes: his and hers. He settled one around my shoulders, and the cold quickly became just another thing not to worry about for the moment. I held my face up to be kissed.

COMING BACK/
GOING FORWARD

I'm so proud of myself for having emerged from depression—maybe not for ever, but for a good long while now. I thought I'd never come out the other side. Even though I wanted to stay curled up and morose, I persevered: I got up almost every morning, washed my face, brushed my teeth, made my bed, poached an egg. Tiny steps, but forward movement. And I got proactive with my psychiatrist. I urged him to tweak my medications because I refused to believe that my fight was over, that this was as good as life gets.

Maybe it's the change in meds, or diligent use of all my coping skills, or maybe it's just plain dumb luck that I've cycled out of depression. Or maybe it's the lovely weather. Who knows? The truth is, one can never be absolutely certain why it comes, or why it goes, despite years of therapy and hard-won insight. Sure, I know my triggers—mostly financial stress and relationship issues these days—and that's valuable information. But it doesn't explain why, out of a pure lucent sky, malaise can suddenly rain down on me.

Now that I feel so much better, it's easier to see the links: oh, that happened, and then I got depressed. But when you're deep inside it, you can see only as far as the gloom will allow. That's what loved ones are for: to remind you of the light. Otherwise, I might believe I'm being punished when I relapse—that I've somehow done wrong, and this is the price I must pay. Nonsense, I know. But many things seem true in depression that are actually phantom pain, wounds from the past. It can be hard to let them go.

That's why the act of witnessing has become so essential to me. It honors what I've been through but puts it back where it belongs: in the past tense. So I always smile when people ask me, "Isn't it traumatic to write about your illness?" Hell, no. It gives me a sense of control, even mastery over what I've endured. I've learned so much from watching my own journey. Experience has given me awareness, and I think that awareness has saved my life.

On a good day, like this luxuriant spring afternoon, I even believe that I command my illness. I believe I'm in charge of my feelings and reactions—that I have the freedom of choice to make my own mistakes, or to do the right thing. Is this the hubris of hypomania speaking? No, I think it's the way other people feel, who aren't beset by mental illness: like their lives are theirs to control.

What an extraordinary feeling! What a gift! To know, even for a while, anticipation when I wake up in the morning and gratitude when I end the day. It's all I ask for. I'm not after feeling high, or giddily manic: all I want is a reprieve from overwrought emotions. The most splendid thing on this earth, I've learned, isn't joy. It's the cessation of pain.

I notice a quiet in my mind, which had clamored with cruel, nasty thoughts not so very long ago. Now I see a swarm of bees around a branch of bougainvillea, and I don't think they're there to sting me. I watch a squirrel run up a tree in my backyard, and I don't once notice his resemblance to a rat. Life is not all romance and roses, but the sun is warm on my face and when I close my eyes to enjoy it, no chilling thoughts intrude.

I tiptoe around my newfound respite, afraid to disturb it or scare it away. I wonder where it's headed, but that's just a passing thought that I'm able to brush away like the bee that ventures too close to me. I wish I could say without any doubt whatsoever why I was shackled for so long, and why those chains no longer bind me. But I don't waste my freedom trying to figure it out. There's no definitive answer, and I know it. There's only this mercy, and this April afternoon.

— — —

THE PAST IS JUST
THE BEGINNING

I used to ruminate—sometimes I still do—about who I was before I was diagnosed with bipolar disorder. On difficult days, I measure everything against it: What could I do back then that I can't do now? I used to be able to work around the clock. I used to have a photographic memory. I used to hop on a helicopter to Catalina for the weekend. The past is like schmutz on a black cashmere sweater—I try to shake it off, but it's too tenacious. I'm haunted by my used-to-be's.

The other day I ran into a lawyer I knew from my former law firm in Beverly Hills. He was a young associate then; I was his unofficial mentor. I taught him traditional ways to cheat without getting into trouble—by using old forms instead of thinking new thoughts, for example, or billing out every phone call at a minimum quarter of an hour. Little tricks of the lucrative trade, which had been passed down to me and which I gratefully used. By virtue of our teacher/student relationship, I was his *de facto* superior, and that was understood between us.

No more. He was dressed in muted elegance: an Italian gray-green suit and loafers with little gold "G" buckles, whispering their provenance. I could almost smell the rich dark leather of his briefcase, which was weathered to perfection. Understatement like that doesn't come cheap; in fact, he reeked of success. I, on the other hand, had just emerged from my writing café, where I'd spent several annoying hours wrestling with intransigent verbs. My seen-better-days sweater was rumpled, the elbows nearly worn through. My jeans had a hole in the knee that wasn't intended as a fashion statement.

We exchanged the usual opening salvos, then got down to the grit of it:

"Are you married?" he asked.

I shook my head no. He showed me a picture of his wife.

"Kids?"

"Um, no." More photos: twins.

"Where are you working now?" he asked.

I pointed to the little café, and he didn't understand. "That's where I go to write," I said.

"Oh," he said. A beat. "I remember you always wanted to write. Screenplays?"

Hah! I rattled off my standard line: "I wrote a memoir that to my astonishment became a *New York Times* bestseller." It was my brief shining moment in the sun, and I wanted to savor it, knowing all too well what would happen next.

"Really?" he said. "What's it called?"

And there it was again, that damned title that continues to out me. I thought for a minute of making something else up, then caught a glimpse of myself in the café window. No, never, not for a million dollars. I faced down the devil in Gucci loafers and looked him straight in the eye.

"It's called *Manic*," I said. "About my life with bipolar disorder."

"That's terrific," he said, without a single blink. He always was a good lawyer. "You know, I made partner," he said.

"Congratulations!" I said, and I sort of meant it at the time. After exchanging the obligatory let's-do-lunches, we went our separate ways. I didn't know whether to laugh or cry. Mostly I wanted to feel safe again from uncomfortable encounters. So I returned to the café and sat at my regular seat by the window. "Back so soon?" the waiter asked. "The usual?"

I nodded, then all at once I realized that *this* was now my usual, not that faraway past. And this, too, was about to be my past— this very moment, and all the moments yet to come. There was no chance of holding on to them. They flee as soon as they materialize, like a frosty breath on a winter day. When my waiter came back with my latte, I saw that he'd drawn a big heart in the foam. I smiled. *I'm right where I need to be*, I thought. Here, now, at last.

SECTION VIII

Appendix

RESOURCES

These are resources I've found helpful in my writing and my own recovery:

ORGANIZATIONS

National Alliance on Mental Illness (NAMI)
Website: https://www.nami.org
Facebook: https://www.facebook.com/NAMI
Helpline: 1-800-950-6264
This is one of the primary sources I recommend to the public. It's especially useful for loved ones seeking information and support, and it offers free local support and training groups.

International Bipolar Foundation
Website: https://ibpf.org
Twitter: @IntlBipolar
Phone: 1-858-598-5967
Started by parents of children with bipolar disorder, the foundation is now international in scope. By contacting the website, you can sign up for their My Support newsletter; obtain a copy of their book, *Healthy Living with Bipolar Disorder*; and access expert lectures and archived webinars on fascinating topics.

American Association of Suicidology
Website: https://suicidology.org
A 501(c)(3) nonprofit association dedicated to the understanding and prevention of suicide.

The Mighty

Website: https://themighty.com

Facebook: https://www.facebook.com/MentalHealthOnTheMighty

Twitter: @TheMightySite

A news compendium and support site for the mental health community, also a forum for sharing personal stories.

Alcoholics Anonymous

Website: https://www.aa.org

Twitter: @AlcoholicsAA

A twelve-step program for anyone seeking help with a substance abuse problem. AA is nonprofessional, self-supporting, multiracial, apolitical, and available almost everywhere. There is no age requirement. Help with narcotics abuse is also available at Narcotics Anonymous, https://www.na.org.

Didi Hirsch Mental Health Services

Website: https://didihirsch.org

For mental health or substance use services: 1-888-807-8250

For suicide prevention: 1-800-273-8255

Didi Hirsch provides suicide prevention, mental health, and substance use services to communities where stigma or poverty limits access. Their Suicide Prevention Center in L.A. is the first, and one of the most comprehensive, in the nation.

Depression and Bipolar Support Alliance (DBSA)

Website: https://www.dbsalliance.org

DBSA offers free in-person and online peer support groups for people living with a mood disorder, as well as their friends and family. Parents who have a child living with depression or bipolar disorder can join the online community for parents, the Balanced Mind Parent Network.

Saks Institute for Mental Health Law, Policy, and Ethics

Website: https://gould.usc.edu/faculty/centers/saks/

Founded by acclaimed author, law professor, and MacArthur Genius Grant recipient Elyn Saks, who lives with schizophrenia. Located at USC, the Saks Institute is a think tank and research institute that studies issues at the intersection of law, mental health, and ethics. It also influences policy reform and advocacy actions for improved treatment of people with mental illness.

CRISIS RESOURCES
National Suicide Prevention Lifeline
1-800-273-8255

Crisis Text Line
Website: https://www.crisistextline.org/
Text HOME to 741741

The Trevor Project
Website: https://www.thetrevorproject.org
1-866-488-7386
A nonprofit organization focused on suicide prevention efforts among LGBTQ
  youth.

SAMHSA Helpline (Treatment Referral Routing Service)
Website: https://www.samhsa.gov/find-help/national-helpline
1-800-662-4357
The Substance Abuse and Mental Health Services Administration provides
  referrals to local treatment facilities, support groups, and communi-
  ty-based organizations for individuals with mental health and/or substance
  abuse issues.

Vets4Warriors
Website: https://www.vets4warriors.com
1-855-838-8255
A 24/7 confidential support network committed to ensuring that all veterans,
  service members, their families, and caregivers always have direct and immediate access to a peer who understands their life experiences and the
  challenges they face.

UCLA Dual Diagnosis Program
Website: https://www.semel.ucla.edu/dual-diagnosis-program/Our_Program
Information and admissions: 1-310-983-3598
300 Medical Plaza, Ste. 2400, Los Angeles, CA 90025
An eight-week outpatient program for individuals with co-occurring mental
  illness and substance abuse issues. It includes daily groups, individual therapy, and medication management.

READING AND VIEWING RECOMMENDATIONS

In addition to my own books, *Manic: A Memoir* (about my adult life with bipolar disorder) and *The Dark Side of Innocence: Growing Up Bipolar* (about my childhood), I recommend the following:

Psychology Today: I write an ongoing blog for *Psychology Today* magazine called "The Bipolar Lens," https://www.psychologytoday.com/us/blog/the-bipolar-lens. The magazine's website also offers a terrific "Find a Therapist" resource, https://www.psychologytoday.com/us.

Darkness Visible: A Memoir of Madness, by William Styron

An Unquiet Mind: A Memoir of Moods and Madness, by Kay Redfield Jamison

The Center Cannot Hold: My Journey Through Madness, by Elyn Saks

The Noonday Demon: An Atlas of Depression, by Andrew Solomon

Touched with Fire: Manic-Depressive Illness and the Artistic Temperament, by Kay Redfield Jamison

A Beautiful Mind, by Sylvia Nasar

Electroboy: A Memoir of Mania, by Andy Behrman

The Curious Incident of the Dog in the Night-Time, by Mark Haddon

Beautiful Boy: A Father's Journey Through His Son's Addiction, by David Sheff

Crazy: A Father's Search Through America's Mental Health Madness, by Pete Earley

Loving Someone with Bipolar Disorder, by Julie A. Fast and John D. Preston

The Bipolar Survival Guide: What You and Your Family Need to Know, by David J. Miklowitz, Ph.D.

The Bipolar Child: The Definitive and Reassuring Guide to Childhood's Most Misunderstood Disorder (3d ed.), by Demitri Papolos, M.D., and Janice Papolos

Feeling Good: The New Mood Therapy, by David D. Burns, M.D.

I also recommend two insightful documentaries by director Lisa Klein: *Of Two Minds*, an intimate, sometimes painful, sometimes painfully funny look at bipolar disorder and all those affected by it; and *The S Word*, an exploration of suicide—that most taboo of subjects—through the eyes of people who have been there and are now committed to preventing others from getting to that edge. For information and access, go to https://madpixfilms.com/.

An essay I wrote for the *New York Times*, about bipolar dating and the importance of having the support of loved ones, was adapted for the first season of the highly successful TV series *Modern Love*. Episode 3, called "Take Me As I Am, Whoever I Am," stars Oscar-winning actress Anne Hathaway as me(!). The series streams on Amazon Prime Video.

ACKNOWLEDGMENTS

I DEDICATED THIS BOOK TO Nancy Bacal, my writing teacher, and Dr. Geoffry White, my therapist, because I can hardly remember a time when they weren't on my side, pushing me to go deeper, inspiring me with their wisdom and strength. I gave them many reasons to give up on me, but no one could ask for braver or more persistent champions. My heartfelt thanks also go out to the following:

—To my agent Will Lippincott at Aevitas Creative Management, who has been a dear friend from the first hour I met him, and a true blessing ever since. Thank you for coming into my life;

—To my editor Renée Sedliar, who has shepherded this book with great compassion, humor, and vision. Thank you for seeing its potential and saying yes;

—To Dr. Harvey Sternbach, whose unrivaled expertise, patience, and generosity of heart have never failed me;

—To Karen Kendig Simon of Celebrity Mental Health Speakers, who has always shown such faith in me;

—To Cisca Schreefel, my production editor, and Martha Whitt, my copyeditor, who were so encouraging, warm, and capable while putting my manuscript into final form; and to the whole Hachette Go team, including Alison Dalafave, for making this book a reality;

—To the members, past and present, of Nancy Bacal's inimitable Wednesday morning writing group, especially Marilyn Levine, Kim Kowsky, Ann Bailey, Carla Weber, Lisa Klein, Arnold Pomerantz, Beacon Miodovsky, Kiki Christensen, alums Maureen Miller,

James Fearnley, Soo-Hyun Chung, Nina Asher, and in memoriam, Paul Mantee. What would I do and who would I be without my family?

—To my beloved friends and supporters Robert Young, Juliet Green, John Whelpley, Elyn Saks, Suzy Davis Mantee, Dr. Joan Osder, Ebet Dudley, Terry Hoffmann, Lisa Mattice, Dawn Scherer, Dr. Elizabeth Suti, Dr. Rita Resnick, Francesca McCaffery, Francesca Kimpton, Garett Carlson, and Lori Depp;

—To Le Pain Quotidien in Beverly Hills, for all the table space they let go to waste while I was writing;

—To Anne Hathaway, Dan Jones, and John Carney for bringing my "Modern Love" essay to glorious, if heartbreaking, life;

—To John Trevor Wolff, for a lifetime of knowing who I really am even when I'm not quite sure myself, and for holding that knowledge in trust for me;

—To all my readers who've written to tell me their own stories, give me feedback, encourage me, and let me know I'm not alone. You have no idea how much you've helped, and how much I value your input;

And

—To my father, who never leaves me.

ABOUT THE AUTHOR

ONCE A SUCCESSFUL ENTERTAINMENT LITIGATOR representing celebrities and major motion picture studios, Terri Cheney escaped the practice of law to do what she has always wanted to do: write. She now devotes her advocacy skills to the cause of mental health and is on the boards of several national as well as international organizations. Her *New York Times* essay was the inspiration for Anne Hathaway's portrayal of a bipolar character on the acclaimed Amazon TV series, *Modern Love*. Terri lives in Los Angeles, where, she says, a certain amount of eccentricity seems to be appreciated.